How to Have a Better Relationship with Anybody

by

James Hilt

MOODY PRESS

CHICAGO

D0173551

Library of Congress Cataloging in Publication Data

Hilt, James, 1947-
    How to have a better relationship with anybody.

    1. Interpersonal relations.   2. Conduct of life.
3. Christian ethics.   I. Title.
HM132.H526   1984   248'.4   83-13400
ISBN:0-8024-1661-6
        4 5 6 7 Printing / GB / Year 88 87 86

Printed in the United States of America

How to Have
a Better Relationship
with Anybody

To Karen,
my wife and trusted friend

Contents

Preface

Recently, after watching the highly acclaimed movie *Chariots of Fire,* I read the biography of its main character, Eric Liddell, called "The Flying Scotsman." In the book's preface, the author, Sally Magnusson, explained one of her main goals in researching for her book.

Though a record-breaking gold medalist in the 400 meters in the 1924 Olympics, Eric was portrayed on screen as being humble and unassuming. There was a rich wholesomeness to his character. *But was he,* she questioned, *that way in real life?*

Through extensive research, Ms. Magnusson was pleased to learn that the image presented in the movie reflected the real man. In fact, many of Eric's contemporaries thought he was one of the most Christlike people they knew, primarily because of the way he treated people.

Eric's Christlike treatment of others was especially striking during his forced confinement at Weihsien, a Japanese internment camp during World War II. Here many, including a great number of missionaries, reacted to the camp's pressures by treating others with cold indifference. Many Christians were just as selfish as the others, fueling divisions and strife.

This dismal report deeply distressed me, for I have painfully seen this ugly pattern in many believers' lives, even during normal times. The quality of their relationships is not deemed that important. Consequently, their treatment of others is not tempered by true spirituality.

How would we, I asked myself, *treat others if we were suddenly placed into a camp like the one faced by Eric Liddell? Would an existing but hidden ugliness surge to the surface, causing bitter disputes and strife? Would we turn against each other like so many believers did at Weihsien?*

I was deeply touched and, I might add, relieved to learn that Eric Liddell was different. Instead of fueling the fire of strife, he labored day and night, even when stricken with an agonizing brain tumor, to encourage and strengthen others. When disputes arose, Eric was normally consulted to find a solution. He befriended a Russian prostitute who had been shunned by others. Though the camp atmosphere was filled with backbiting and criticism, no one had a bad word to say about Eric, for he was at his best—kind and loving—with everyone. He was a wonderful agent of healing of minds and relationships in that dismal camp.

Herein lies the main purpose of this book. It is meant to bring healing to our minds and relationships. It is designed to identify and purge forces that divide us so that Christ's love can flow in and through our lives unhindered.

So I encourage you not only to "dig in" for increased understanding but also to adopt, if needed, radical new ways of relating.

My heart-felt gratitude goes out to many people whose loving concern has greatly contributed to my life and the content of this book. These include: my wife, Karen, who has consistently loved, encouraged, and supported me; my dear mother, who, prior to her death, did the same—she modeled the importance of being kind and sensitive to others, especially the downtrodden; my father, who is a real friend—he stressed the importance of showing respect to everyone, regardless of his socio-economic status; my brother, Harry, and sisters, Barb, Vicky, Sandy, and Kerry, who have been a constant source of joy; and my in-laws, George and May Hovda, whose loving acceptance into their warm home has been a great source of encouragement and support. I also thank my friends Phil Scull and David Mains for challenging and encouraging me to stretch.

1

Avoid Bitterness; It's Lethal

While sitting on a bench outside a rustic chapel, I felt deeply troubled. It was the last hour of a long weekend retreat.

What's wrong with me, I thought. *As a youth group leader, I should show Christ's love and understanding. But I can't! What keeps bottling up my mind?*

I groaned an inward prayer: *Jesus, when are you going to step in and do something about this?*

Suddenly, I sensed someone approaching. I glanced up and saw my friend Joe, a church leader in our area.

"How was your weekend?" he asked.

"Rough," I replied. A moment of silence passed while I considered sharing my disappointment.

"Something inside of me stopped me from being myself. And my group suffered as a result," I finally said.

Joe responded sympathetically by describing an incident that had made him bitter, eroding his emotional and spiritual health. As I listened to him, I had a distinct feeling that Christ was speaking through him to me.

Perhaps my emotional distress is linked to bitterness, I thought. *Is there anyone toward whom I feel frequent anger?* I questioned myself.

My mind quickly focused on a friend who had betrayed my

trust. For months, his offense had caused bitter annoyance in the back of my mind.

Some time later, I learned how to get rid of that bitterness—in the next chapter I will share the steps I took—and I sensed a gradual release from bondage. I joyfully rediscovered the sweet inner liberty that had evaded me like a mirage.

Since that experience, I have been intrigued by the causes and eroding effects of bitterness. I am convinced that Satan uses it constantly to crush lives. Yet bitterness is so subtle that many Christians view it as less dangerous than some of the more obvious sins.

Anger may come and go, but unfortunately that is not usually the case with bitterness. Bitter feelings will often remain with a person for years. In fact, in my counseling I have met many people, including the elderly, whose bitterness began in their youth.

That is why the writer of Hebrews aptly referred to it as a "bitter root" (Hebrews 12:15). Like a root, bitterness can grow and spread for years, entangling our attitudes, feelings, and thoughts.

Why do people become bitter? Three major causes exist. First, every person has strong needs to love and be unconditionally loved, to feel worthwhile to himself and to others. Each one of us is equipped with a mental radar screen that detects whether or not those needs are being met. The needs and the radar device are built into us by God.

If a person registers a negative message, he feels cheated and deeply wounded inside. Seeds of anger may then germinate, which, if nourished by further evidences of unmet needs, can grow into a root of bitterness.

A second major cause for bitterness is personal loss. Losing something or someone suddenly may be intolerable, and impossible to accept. Mental revolt occurs, which can cause and then feed the bitterness. Because we live in a hazardous, fallen world, many kinds of losses are possible. Financial loss is an example. An overwhelming wave of bitterness became evident in the wake of the Great Crash of 1929. Unable to accept and endure the sudden reversal of fortune, many people reacted bitterly by ending their own lives. Given our present economic state, perhaps this is a picture of things to come.

Loss of health, whether sudden or gradual, can also precipitate bitterness. What a crushing blow it is to a person's equilibrium to learn that he has a blood disease or cancer leading to great pain and perhaps even death. With one stroke, such a loss can change the whole climate of one's mind, causing intense agitation against God and life itself.

Loss of meaning in life is a further possible cause of bitterness. Many people count on finding meaning in life solely by amassing important achievements, but sadly at the expense of cultivating a personal, love-relationship with Christ. For a season, a certain level of satisfaction may be reached. But then, before long, the Law of Diminishing Returns sets in.

Such people eventually reach the point where the more time and energy they invest in achievements, the less, in proportion, they receive in terms of meaning. Disillusionment and bitterness then emerge toward life for promising so much, yet delivering so little.

I do not suggest that achievements should not be pursued. Achievements surely are important and can bring continued joy when they are in accordance with God's will. But building a friendship with Christ must be placed at the top of our list of priorities. Only then will He enrich our lives with a lasting sense of meaning.

Several losses occurring simultaneously are especially apt to provoke bitterness. Consider Job. Having lost his dear children, livestock, and health, he cried out: "I loathe my very life: therefore I will give free rein to my complaint and speak out in the bitterness of my soul" (Job 10:1).

In addition to unmet needs and personal losses, sinful attitudes can also cause bitterness. It is interesting that God so created human beings that when sinful attitudes such as envy, jealousy, and pride emerge in our lives, we are drawn down a path leading to bitterness.

It is evident that jealousy and pride triggered King Saul's bitterness. Following David's conquest of Goliath, women from different cities visited Saul. In a festive mood, they played musical instruments and sang, "Saul has slain his thousands, and David his tens of thousands" (1 Samuel 18:7).

Immediately, Saul burned with jealousy and wounded pride, both of which triggered bitterness. He found it intolerable that some young, unknown sheepherder could detract from his own glorious popularity among the people.

I am familiar with a Christian organization in which several staff members scrupulously critiqued each other's performance with questions such as: Who is most popular? Who holds the highest esteem in the eyes of others? And who is most spiritual?

The ones who seemed to be on the losing end of this win/lose contest of personalities erupted with jealousy, obviously toward the deemed winners. Bitterness then crept in, causing crude power struggles for authority, control, and popularity. Sadly, this contaminated their relationships and sabotaged the overall success of the organization.

Examining our reactions in view of these three major sources of bitterness should help us to identify any existing bitterness in our own lives. Bitterness usually has one or more objects. It is usually directed toward another person, God, and/or oneself. Let's explore this, beginning with other people.

A bitter reaction might normally erupt toward another person when we feel betrayed, hurt, or offended by him. His chosen actions and words—or even the lack of them—can leave us feeling wounded, then angry, then bitter.

That happened to Ben, a college student. In counseling, it became clear that he had longed for unconditional love from his parents—love without any strings attached. Coupled with this was a constant hunger for parental approval, especially from his father. Yet Ben's cravings remained unsatisfied.

Though his father was a committed Christian and a pastor, Ben was bombarded with nonverbal messages like: "*If* you get good grades, excel in sports, and especially prove to be a good Christian model, *then* I will love and accept you. *Then* you will be OK." Thus, in Ben's mind, his acceptability in his father's eyes depended on which certain performance levels he reached. Because everything had to be earned, everything was conditional. Consequently, always having to prove himself—always having to do a tap dance—Ben felt cheated and deeply wounded inside, begetting bitterness, especially toward his father.

All too often, I come across people like Ben, who have been emotionally abused by conditional love from parents and others; we find this frequently, even in Christian homes. Such people have been torn apart inside by a love that was not secure, not in a water-tight compartment, not a gift, and therefore unlike Christ's (see Romans 15:7; 1 John 4:7-12).

For some, God is another object of bitterness. The possible reasons for this are many. For example, bitterness can emerge toward God from cultivating a distasteful, twisted image of Him. Let me explain.

Those holding any belief in God naturally try to construct a mental image of Him. To create this picture, impressions are drawn from a variety of experiences. Each new impression acts like a successive brush stroke on a painting, adding new colors and lines until a certain image takes shape.

As part of this process, a person has a strong tendency to see God like his natural father. In other words, he tends to superimpose the image held toward him, good or bad, onto God. If, therefore, he had a good father figure, he most likely will hold a healthy, positive image of God as well.

On the other hand, if his father appeared repulsive, God will probably also be seen as repulsive. Those whose fathers are usually emotionally distant tend to feel that God is also distant. Those whose fathers are oppressive tend to feel that God is oppressive. Whatever the negative connection, constant misreadings of God's real intents and nature then occur, precipitating bitterness toward Him.

Thinking again of Ben, because his father's love was conditional and fickle, he saw God's love the same way. Having superimposed his father's image onto God, Ben perceived God as a celestial killjoy, who harshly demanded perfection but could never bring Himself to say: "I love you, Ben. I accept you. You are pleasing to Me."

Thus, instead of basking in the rays of Christ's lovingkindness and thankfully serving Him in response to it, Ben felt that God's love had a price tag. It had to be earned. But he never knew when he had done enough.

Finally, Ben concluded that he could never measure up in Christ's eyes, that God was always angry and frustrated with his poor track record. Futility consequently set in, along with intense anger: "I can't do anything right! And that's where You come in, God. You sure blew it when You made me! You're cruel. So You go Your way, and I'll go mine!"

Personal loss has been shown to be a major source of bitterness. When loss occurs, many people blame God for either allowing or causing it. "God, doesn't Your power permit You to control everything? Why, then, did this happen? Where's all of this love and mercy we hear so much about?"

What such people overlook is that many losses are not God's responsibility but result from ill-choices made by us or others, which actually run against the grain of God's will. For example, losses resulting from a painful divorce are never part of His plan for marriage.

Surely, some losses occur unexpectedly, through no fault of our own, such as severe illness or the death of a loved one. And it is at such times that Christ especially empathizes with us. Far beyond our human comprehension, He has suffered tremendous personal loss. Two thousand years ago, Christ underwent excruciating mental pain on the cross, while agonizing, in some eternal sense, over the loss of His own Father's love and intimacy. Every day thousands are eternally lost to His enemy. So God knows all about the pain caused by personal loss. He can empathize with us.

The third possible object of bitterness is oneself. Bitterness can be directed inward as well as toward others and God. What accounts for this? Self-directed bitterness usually occurs when we relentlessly blame ourselves for failing miserably. Though confession might follow, we nevertheless persist in assaulting ourselves, instead of breathing in God's forgiveness and then directing it inward. Instead of treating ourselves as Christ did, with kindness and patience, we brutalize ourselves.

Another cause of self-directed bitterness is the life-style centered on lusts. The creed "If it feels good, do it," without considering the consequences for oneself and others, has been adopted by many. Yet, the human mind is so designed that when lusts rule a person's heart, he can come to detest himself. This usually results from the eventual awareness that an indulgent life leads to boredom, degradation, and dishonor. Worse still is the person's realization that his selfish pursuits have left others deeply scarred along the way.

Bitterness toward self can also emerge from the way a person was raised. Especially when we are young, there exists a strong, instinctual drive to discover who we are, to capture our identity. And our self-image is largely shaped by how we perceive significant people like parents, siblings, peers, and teachers viewing us.

Parents play a key role here. We draw major conclusions about ourselves through their eyes. More specifically, verbal and non-verbal messages are recorded from our parents onto our "parent tape." What is recorded are the perceived meanings behind their attitudes, gestures, words, and actions.

Then, having made this recording, we play the tape over and over in our minds, thereby feeding ourselves the same messages we have received from our parents. As a result, we tend to treat and view ourselves as they did. In view of this, if a person's parent tape is filled with negative, unrealistic messages about him, then he may treat and view himself in ways that create self-directed bitterness.

To clarify what I mean, think again of Ben. Having recorded and then replayed conditional messages received from his parents, he could not unconditionally accept himself, nor identify his

God-given value. And since everything—his parents' love, God's view of him, and his own self-concept—seemed to depend on success, it was either "do or die" in every win/lose situation.

Because so much was emotionally at stake with every challange, namely his parents' acceptance, God's acceptance, and self-acceptance, Ben revolted at the slightest hint of defeat, triggering intense self-directed criticism, leading to self-rejection and then self-directed bitterness.

In counseling, Ben discovered that the harsh suggestions recorded from the past could be erased and replaced by new messages from his eternal Father. These recorded, God-sent messages could then be replayed in his mind, replacing the self-rejection with self-acceptance.

More specifically, Ben came to see that Christ unconditionally loved him and that His love was secure, in a water-tight compartment (Psalm 36:5-10; Romans 5:8; 1 John 4). Moreover, Christ showed His grace, or unconditional acceptance, toward him (Romans 15:7; 1 Timothy 1:14). Ben began to realize that there are no conditions and no hidden agendas to receiving God's love and acceptance. They are gifts, wonderful gifts, and can only be received as gifts. God's love is like sunlight: a person can do nothing to either lessen or intensify its power, but only bask in its warmth!

Ben learned that even if he were totally paralyzed, God's loving acceptance of him would be no less than if he became a missionary to Africa. For God's love and acceptance are not based on any performance levels reached, but rather on His own character. Along with this, Ben soon realized that God had made him into a unique, special person. Though sometimes beset with sin, he was not a worthless worm but possessed immeasurable value because God had placed it there. As stated in Psalm 139:14: "I am fearfully and wonderfully made."

Next, Ben discovered that he could treat and view himself as Christ did. Because God was kind to and patient with him, he could be kind to and patient with himself. Because Christ gave him the gift of unconditional love and grace (unconditional acceptance), he could unconditionally accept himself. He could give the gift of grace to himself, enabling him to become, like Stephen, "full of God's grace and power" (Acts 6:8).

Now, as a result, with these truths branded in Ben's mind, especially the promise of God's unconditional love, there is much less emotionally at stake when facing new tasks, making him feel less threatened and more relaxed. God's grace has become sufficient (2 Corinthians 12:9).

"But didn't Ben become self-centered?" you might ask. No. Just the opposite occurred. You see, there is a big difference between the self-acceptance found in Christ and the self-centered pride found in ourselves. The realization that we are accepting something that God made—that we had no hand in our own creation—breeds humility.

I enjoy the beautiful painting of the Swiss Alps hanging in my office. But there is no way I could become haughty about it, for I did not paint it. Likewise, how can we become arrogant about something that God, in His power and wisdom, designed and created?

So Ben grew in humility. And because the emotional pain of past rejections and self-rejection was healed, he gained newfound freedom to serve God and others. Not only that, but Ben's drive to serve Christ grew, not from striving to earn His love but out of deep gratitude for having received it as a gift already! Thus, godly self-acceptance is not synonymous with egotistical pride. Rather, it breeds humility and frees a person up to a life of joyous service!

But bitterness acts like an acid or cancer, eating away at our emotional, physical, and spiritual health. It also crushes relationships. This happens mostly because, when infected, the mind instinctively focuses on one reaction, revenge.

When bitter, the mind draws upon its resources to plan and initiate acts of vengeance. This process acts like a nation's mobilization of its human and material resources to successfully wage war against its enemy. That is why so many words and actions are heavily laced with attack overtones. As we said before, bitterness can be held toward others, God, and oneself. Revenge can be leveled at any of these, operating on either a conscious or unconscious level. Let's explore examples in connection with all three.

When a person feels hurt or is offended by another person, and reacts with bitterness, he then searches for ways to get even. The means available to him are almost unlimited and include: character assassination, cheating, gossip, lying, name-calling, physical and verbal attacks, withdrawal, and withholding love. Whatever means the wronged person chooses, he needs to employ much creativity and savvy to maximize the pain in the other person.

Several years ago, Dick joined the Bible study and sharing group to which I belonged. Since he was a new believer, he was full of questions—refreshing questions—some of which inspired everyone to grow. The acceptance and warmth that Dick received helped him quickly to feel like a part of our group.

Several months later another person, Ted, joined our group. He also added new dimensions to it, but for different reasons. Ted's refreshing bluntness encouraged some others to strip away their masks. He had a way of helping others to be themselves.

Unfortunately, from the onset, Dick did not share the group's acceptance of Ted. Someone new was getting attention, and that made Dick feel less wanted. But he was wrong, because both of them were warmly received.

Consequently, stirred with jealousy, Dick became embittered toward Ted. Wanting to attack, he shunned him. Whenever Ted spoke up, Dick acted aloof and bored. Even hearing Ted's name in conversation made him feel uncomfortable. And because Dick never brought himself to accept Ted, he became soured on the whole group, to the point of leaving it altogether. For this and other reasons, Dick's unresolved bitterness hurt him more than anyone else.

In the past, when I was counseling disturbed, rebellious youth, I noticed that alcohol and drugs could be used as weapons. Many young people plunge into the drug world to scream at their parents: "Your love for me is so shallow! You act as if I count for nothing. So what difference does it make if I destroy myself? Now suffer!" Then, as they detect the pain their retaliative plan induces, they feel a twisted sense of satisfaction, which drives them even further into the dark world of drugs, irresponsibility, and self-centeredness.

Mental disorders can also provide the means for a bitter attack against another person. At first glance, such weapons may appear weak and ineffective. But they can be very potent in their pain-inducing power, as attested to by many.

Let me illustrate. Joan lived in a family full of achievers. Though she met every task with determination, she always felt lower than her more intelligent brothers and sisters.

Sadly, Joan's parents did not affirm her strong efforts, nor what she did right. Instead, they bombarded her with statements like: "Your report card shows B's while your brothers and sisters get mostly A's. Why can't you be more like them?"

By the time Joan left high school, it had dawned on her that she could never be exactly like the others in her family. In her parents' eyes, she would always fall short. Consequently, she turned against them with bitterness and fierce wrath.

I'll show them, Joan thought. *Since they think I'm such a dud,*

I'll give them my worst. Then they'll really have something to worry about. She began filling her mind with bizarre, irrational thoughts, which, over a period of time, became deeply entrenched patterns.

Joan withdrew her contact from people and created a fantasy world—a seemingly safe world—in which her needs supposedly could be met. She acted and spoke as she pleased regardless of how it affected others. Her actions tormented both of her parents with intense guilt and despair. Sadly, many mental disorders are bitter attacks on others. That is why so many disturbed people are angry and manipulative.

I might add that gnawing guilt also destroyed Joan's emotional health. Always feeling lower than her brothers and sisters (and, therefore, defeated in her parents' eyes), Joan carried a great burden of guilt. But hers was false guilt, guilt that God did not want her to have.

True moral guilt results from the Holy Spirit's conviction of sin in our lives. It is a signal from God indicating that something is wrong and in need of repair. To resolve true guilt, we must engage in "spiritual breathing." First, we exhale, confessing our sins. Next, we inhale, breathing in God's forgiveness, which enables us to forgive ourselves. Spiritual breathing complies with 1 John 1:9, which reads: "If we confess our sins, he is faithful and just and will forgive us our sins and purify us from all unrighteousness."

False guilt, in contrast, does not find its source in God's wise judgments but in wrong conclusions caused by faulty thinking or destructive suggestions from others. Thus, unlike true guilt, it does not contain a redemptive quality. Instead, false guilt only crushes and scars. Moreover, spiritual breathing does not resolve it. Rather, it must be recognized as false and then discarded.

Because of her parents' constant comparisons and unrealistic expectations, Joan always felt plagued by guilt (false guilt), even when trying her best. Consequently, in an effort to atone for that guilt, she tried to punish herself by causing, on a conscious and unconscious level, the onslaught of emotional upheaval. Thus, this drive for atonement, coupled with the bitter attacks leveled at her parents, caused the described emotional distress.

Parents can avoid the kinds of pressures placed on Joan by emphasizing to their children that, in God's eyes, real success comes from building strong Christian character. For here there are no win/lose situations. Because we can all become more like Christ, we can all win!

That is just a sample of how attacks of bitterness can be leveled at others. Everywhere we see Satan destroying churches, homes, people, and relationships. And revenge plays a very strategic role in his vicious plans.

God is the second possible object of bitter attack, for unbelievers and believers alike. Often, unbelievers raised in Christian homes will avoid anything smelling of Christianity, because, tragically, they have been taught that God is much quicker to judge than to love. They know He exists. But because God appears to them to be so negative and brutal, they choose to avoid Him and His commandments as a means of bitter protest. For many, the response is to embrace hedonistic, materialistic life-styles.

When bitter at God, some believers strike out at Him as well. In fact, sometimes their attacks are harsher than those of un-believers, especially when they draw the conclusion that God does not have their best in mind. Recently, I talked with a believer who had been asking God for a marriage partner for months. But because this had not materialized, he mentally revolted against the Lord; then he began searching for friends in bars, in an effort to get even with God.

Further means of striking out at God include: criticizing other believers and Christian beliefs, cutting off church attendance and involvement, and living a double life with one foot in the church and the other in the world.

In addition to others and God, bitter attacks can also be leveled at oneself as a result of self-directed bitterness. Several years ago, I worked with a young person whose parents were killed in a freak car accident. After the accident, Stan unwittingly drew the conclusion that his parents' deaths were his fault. He blamed himself, even though his was clearly false guilt—guilt that God did not want him to have.

Consequently, Stan's self-directed bitterness grew, and he developed a vendetta against himself. Such self-directed attacks, coupled with a drive to punish himself in his effort to atone for the guilt, forced Stan to cut off every source of happiness. He dropped his close friends and began to drink.

Through counseling, Stan came to realize that his was not true guilt requiring confession, but rather false guilt. That realization enabled him to discard it. His self-directed bitterness was also healed through the four steps described in the next chapter. Stan's healing freed him up to rekindle interest in other people and life itself.

Self-directed attacks can harm us, not only emotionally and

socially as in Stan's case, but physically as well, and even without our awareness of it. That is because bitterness, operating on an unconscious level, can activate certain dysfunctional impulses or signals in the nervous system which, over a period of time, can cause physical problems. Some cases of high blood pressure, ulcers, and other ailments are the products of this process.

Physical harm can result from conscious decisions as well. Suicide is the most potent way of getting even with oneself. Because it is so final, it represents the ultimate form of self-directed attack.

Further means of self-directed attacks include: incessant self-criticism, belittling oneself in the presence of others, excessive alcohol or drug intake, and setting oneself up for emotional, social, or vocational failure. Any means that contains a self-destructive element might be employed.

Thus we can see that bitter attacks, whether aimed at others, God, or oneself, can be lethal. Such attacks set into motion powerful forces of destruction. Those who are plagued by bitterness, therefore, need to be healed.

Note: Several paragraphs in this chapter were reprinted by permission from *Christian Life*, copyright September 1976, Christian Life, Inc., 396 E. St. Charles Rd., Wheaton, IL 60187. I wrote the article "Bitterness Can Be Overcome."

2
Dig Out the Root of Bitterness

If we came across a large venomous snake in our path, most of us would go to great lengths to avoid it. Yet, we so often do just the opposite when we meet bitterness, although its venom poisons a person's system. We allow large injections to penetrate us, setting into motion raw forces that can ruin our health and relationships.

It distresses me that so many people have been struck by it. Some Christians are the most bitter people I know. Bitterness is presently poisoning the Body of Christ, providing our common enemy with strategic strongholds from which to stir up division and strife.

Thus, the Body of Christ desperately needs a mass healing of bitterness. I contend that such an event could ignite another great awakening comparable to the one that was witnessed during Edwards, Wesley, and Whitefield's time. Without bitterness, fresh torrents of love would gush forth among believers, offering the world a clearer picture of what Christ-centered love and fellowship are all about.

Are you bitter? Has any bitterness taken root toward others, God, or yourself? List on a sheet of paper the names of those people toward whom you are bitter.

Perhaps bitterness has bound you for years. You think that time has taken care of it. But, instead, like a ball that has been forced underwater, the bitterness has merely been pushed down deep inside your life. In other words, it was buried alive and still needs true liquidation.

If you are embittered, dig out that "bitter root" (Hebrews 12:15). Heed Paul's words: "Get rid of all bitterness" (Ephesians 4:31). Here are four steps that, followed closely, will bring the needed healing.

1. CONFESS THE BITTERNESS AS SIN TO CHRIST.

Perhaps you have suffered a great loss or been deeply wounded by another person. Nevertheless, do not try to justify your reaction or explain it away. First, you must recognize that a bitter reaction is always a sinful reaction and can never be rationalized away. Bitterness always needs to be confessed to God, regardless of its cause. When you have confessed the sin, be sure to breathe in God's forgiveness, which He promised (see 1 John 1:9).

2. ASK GOD FOR THE POWER TO FULLY ACCEPT THE SOURCE OF THE BITTERNESS. ASK HIM TO HELP YOU REMOVE THE MENTAL REVOLT, THE INWARD STEWING IN CONNECTION WITH IT.

Often our minds fixate on what has hurt or offended us. Its memory is replayed incessantly. But that only narrows the field of consciousness, driving away positive, wholesome thoughts. So instead of mentally replaying the offense like a record, take the needle off.

Sound difficult, or even impossible? I understand. Sometimes we are truly powerless to accept certain blows or setbacks in life. That is why only God is able to grant the power to accept them. And the only way for us to receive that power is to ask Him for it.

By acceptance, however, I do not mean to suggest that we must somehow relish our hurt or count it as good. Many of our afflictions result from evil forces in the world and should never be seen as anything less than evil. Acceptance is not the same as approval.

Nor should God be thanked for the offense. Sometimes we are told to praise God for everything. I strongly disagree with this statement. How can we praise Him for evil itself such as adultery, cheating, mental or physical brutality? To do so accuses God of being the culprit and severely distorts His image! As seen throughout Scripture, God detests and is angered by all evil. And we must detest it too. He should never be praised for anything of a fallen or evil nature.

Christ can be thanked, however, for the way He can work even through evil to bring about good in our lives (Romans 8:28). For example, young Joe's parents constantly fought. The fighting led to divorce, something never intended by God. Instead, this deeply grieved Him.

God, however, worked through Joe's tragic home life to make him sensitive and understanding toward the struggles of others, thereby bringing good out of a raw situation. Thus, there is a big difference between praising God for evil and thanking Him for faithfully bearing fruit through it.

Paul Tournier, the noted Christian counselor and writer, put it this way: "Accepting suffering, bereavement, and disease does not mean taking pleasure in them, steeling oneself against them, or hoping that distractions or the passage of time will make us forget them. It means offering them to God so that He can make them bring forth fruit."[1]

Furthermore, acceptance is not synonymous with indifference or mental resignation. Sometimes Christ directs us to eliminate the trouble spot, as Paul did with the accusations leveled at him from Corinth. At other times, we are told to keep still, as Christ did before Pilate. Whatever direction we might receive, we must patiently endure. But such an endurance is active, not passive.

Acceptance of our suffering frees us up to tap into God's best resources to go on and initiate change when we're told to do so. Christ then has more to work with to restore us and to bring about any needed resolution. Our pains can be used to advance the kingdom.

Consider the apostle Paul. His sufferings were great. His mental state of acceptance, however, allowed him to endure and serve instead of reacting with bitterness. God could then sustain him and work through his pains to shake the Roman Empire.

Not only does God want us to accept the pains of the past and present, but future ones as well. In the Garden of Gethsemane, Christ foresaw the soon-to-come fist blows to the face from burly Roman soldiers, the crown of thorns, the burning nails, and the heartless mockings. Worse still was the prospect of His Father's separation from Him. And, as seen through His blood-like sweat, everything inside of Him recoiled at it all. But Christ accepted His hour of darkness in advance, knowing that it would unleash awesome spiritual forces for good in the world. Upheld by God's grace, we can do the same.

3. ASK CHRIST FOR THE POWER TO FORGIVE EVERYONE WHO HAS

---

1. Paul Tournier, *The Healing of Persons* (New York: Harper & Row, 1965).

OFFENDED YOU—THOSE WHOSE ACTIONS PRECIPITATED THE BIT-
TERNESS.

Notice in Ephesians 4 that, following the command in verse 31
to "get rid of all bitterness, rage, and anger," Paul proceeded to
add in verse 32: "Be kind and compassionate to one another,
forgiving each other, just as in Christ God forgave you" (italics
added).

Before we can show compassion and kindness to our offenders,
we must exercise forgiveness. But relying solely on our own
human resources, we are powerless to do this according to God's
specifications. That is why we must ask Christ for the power to
forgive. He alone holds the key.

"But the person who hurt me doesn't deserve to be forgiven,"
you might say. "He hasn't even said he's sorry." Forgive him in
your mind, anyway. If he has truly wronged you and not yet
repented, he still bears his guilt. He is still accountable to God.

We must remember that forgiveness releases the pressure of
steam that can otherwise build up, causing great mental stress. It
is a wonderful therapeutic device, which cleanses, heals, and
brings increased love, peace, and strength to the mind. Forgiveness is therefore not a grudging burden, but an experience of
relief and joy.

So forgive each person by name. If self-directed bitterness
exists, do not hold a grudge against yourself. Forgive yourself as
well.

Following forgiveness, the question is usually asked: Should I
tell my offender he's been forgiven? It all depends on Christ's
specific will. In prayer ask Him to reveal it to you. In response,
Christ might direct you to approach this person and verbally
make amends, knowing this would maximize healing and recon-
ciliation. On the other hand, He might lead you to remain silent,
knowing that speaking up would do more harm than good.
Whatever direction you receive, trust that it will serve the
greatest good.

4. ASK CHRIST TO HEAL YOU OF ALL THE BITTERNESS HELD TOWARD
OTHERS, GOD, OR YOURSELF FROM YOUR PAST AND PRESENT.

Allow Him to dig up all of the bitterness that has perhaps been
growing and entangling your life like a root for years. The entire
"bitter root" must be removed, if complete healing is to occur.
Only Christ can remove all of your bitterness—past and present—and give you a new attitude and outlook.

Confession, acceptance, forgiveness, and healing—obviously,
those are simple steps. But used by the Spirit of God, they are

power-packed! For years I have led many individuals, married couples, and groups through those four steps in prayer, which often resulted in remarkable transformations of minds and relationships. Sometimes during prayer, people discover an immediate and total release from bitterness. They describe a newfound freedom from bondage—something that had bound them for days, months, or years.

Such was the experience of several people already mentioned, including Ben. After asking God to release him from the bitterness he held toward his parents, God, and himself, Ben sensed an immediate release from his bondage. Before long, his vengeful feelings and acts leveled at his parents gave way to a new compassion for them. Ben began to see his father in a new light, which compelled him to open up lines of communication with him.

Along with this, Ben stopped reacting bitterly against God and began to build a new image of and relationship with Him. Instead of viewing Christ as an oppressive tyrant, he began to see Him as a trusted Friend.

As a result of being healed of self-directed bitterness, Ben no longer sought revenge against himself. No longer did he set himself up for personal failure. Rather, he pursued godly self-acceptance (as described in chapter 1), replacing the self-directed harshness with self-directed kindness.

Although the feeling of release is immediate for some, others may require more time. Some people may need days or weeks before they can acknowledge all of the names of those toward whom they hold bitterness. In such cases, they must undergo the four steps more than once.

Whether the release is immediate or slow in coming, I have great confidence in God's response to the honest prayer for healing. Surely, God "heals the brokenhearted and binds up their wounds" (Psalm 147:3).

Following your prayer and Christ's response of healing, be on guard against every temptation to pick up the bitterness again. Satan would like nothing better than to drag you back into the same pit. To prevent this danger, deal quickly and wisely with your anger. "Do not let the sun go down while you are still angry" (Ephesians 4:26). Remember that unresolved anger has a way of turning into bitterness.

Moreover, each time you feel wounded inside or offended by another person, do not allow mental revolt to set in. Instead, ask God for the power to accept and forgive on the spot. As a result, you will cultivate an accepting, forgiving spirit, which will prevent you from becoming embittered by the pains of this world.

Periodically throughout this book, bitterness will be examined. If at any point you identify a bitter root in your life, be sure to undergo the four described steps. As you do so, your mind and your relationships will be healed.

3

Risk Saying, "You're Special"

Following their home Bible study, Jill rises to leave the Andersons' house. As they stand near the door, she feels a sudden surge of love and warmth for the Andersons. Jill feels a strong impulse to throw her arms around this couple and say, "You know, your encouragement and sensitivity mean a lot. See, you really mean a lot to me." However, just as she begins to speak, a voice inside cautions her, *Oh, Jill, wouldn't that be foolish?* So, instead, she merely says, "Say, it was a good study tonight, wasn't it?"

On her way home, Jill continues to savor the intimacy felt throughout the night. *But isn't it sad,* she thinks, *that I couldn't bring myself to tell them how I really feel about them?*

Sound familiar? How often have you felt a strong impulse to say to a cherished friend: "You know, I really like you," or, "I think you're special"? These words almost pour out when another voice warns, *Keep still. Don't be silly. Stay cool.* And to play it safe, you comply. Your kind and encouraging thoughts remain unspoken.

Afterward, you continue to bask in the glow of that friendship. But then you wonder why it was so difficult to express your real feelings. Perhaps this occurred the last time you saw your parents, or while sitting across from your wife or husband in a restaurant.

Surely, many different reasons could account for this choking. But here are three major ones. First, there is fear of embarrassment, to oneself and to others. Saying, "You mean a lot," may sound like a good idea initially. But then that inner voice tells you: *He won't take me seriously. He'll think I'm being melodramatic and overly sentimental. He may even laugh. Or I may make him feel self-conscious and uneasy. He won't know how to respond. Better keep my real feelings inside. Why put him or me on the spot?* So on go the brakes!

A second major reason that this message remains unspoken is the fear of vulnerability. Whenever such affirming expressions are given, the relationship might assume deeper intimacy, requiring more expressions of mutual interest and commitment.

Although this prospect might appeal to many, others recoil inside at the whole idea. Many people feel compelled to keep a certain emotional distance in every relationship. "Getting close" is forbidden territory. Why? Many people fear getting hurt. They realize that the stronger the tie is, the greater the pain will be if that relationship backfires. Thus, playing it safe, they refuse to set themselves up for emotional pain and social failure. So they hide their real feelings, even from those closest to them.

A third reason many people bury their feelings from others is because they have adopted society's values. Our culture glorifies independence, self-sufficiency, and toughness. People therefore avoid doing or saying anything that might detract from the "bionic" image they hope to convey. This includes "you mean a lot to me" kinds of expressions. In their minds, such expressions convey softness and weakness.

We see this mentality especially in men. Society teaches us that an all-powerful, rough-and-tough exterior is essential to masculinity. And because many men feel that expressing their real feelings would betray their manhood, they never say to their wives, "Dear, you're special. I love you"—even when their wives are starving for signs of affection! This, I might add, is one major reason many hate-campaigns on the part of women have emerged toward men. Too many wives have given from their hearts to their husbands—they have sacrificed, pouring out labors of love to all family members—only to see their husbands become increasingly unaffectionate and self-centered.

Committed to their self-indulgences, these men never affirm their wives for their many labors; they do not convey warmth. Then, feeling betrayed, hurt, and embittered, their wives react with revenge, sometimes generalizing ill-feelings toward all men. How different many women would feel and act today if their husbands assumed their God-given roles and showed them warmth and affection!

Having provided three major reasons people often bury the described feelings of affection and encouragement, I want to compare their relationships to the example of the apostle Paul, who, in my mind, was one of the most courageous and toughest characters recorded in history.

The Philippian church was very dear to Paul's heart. It was the first church founded in Europe on his second missionary journey, and it supported him when he moved on to Thessalonica. Thus, because the Philippian believers were so special to Paul, he let them know his real feelings in a letter. "For God is my witness, how I long for you all with the affection of Christ Jesus" (Philippians 1:8, NASB*). Later on in the same letter, he added, " . . . my beloved brethren whom I long to see, my joy and crown" (4:1, NASB).

Someone might protest, "But isn't it less threatening to express such feelings to a large group of people, as Paul did, than to one person? Politicians do it all the time." Granted, the anonymity of a large group might make it easier to offer such expressions. But when Paul wrote this letter, he pictured individuals, not a mass of people. As he wrote, familiar faces probably came to mind.

Besides, Paul spoke the same way to individuals. For example, in his second letter to Timothy (1:3-4), he said, "I thank God . . . as night and day I constantly remember you in my prayers. Recalling your tears, I long to see you, so that I may be filled with joy." Here Paul was saying: I thank God for you, Timothy. I think and pray about you night and day. I long to see you again. And your presence fills me with joy.

Obviously, Timothy meant a lot to Paul. And I believe that Paul expressed such feelings to many people, not just Timothy. For people filling churches everywhere were special to him.

But wasn't Paul afraid of embarrassing himself or others? Didn't he worry about being vulnerable? What about appearing soft and weak?

Paul had such compassion for people that he could not suppress his real feelings for them. He would have "burst at the seams" if he had tried. People and their walks with Christ were so important to Paul that he had to express how special they were and how much they meant to him. Paul's drive to do that was so

*New American Standard Bible.

great that embarrassment to himself and to others was not even an issue with him.

Nor was fear of vulnerability. Having poured his life into others, Paul knew all too well what it meant to be betrayed and hurt. His wounds ran deep. Nevertheless, he refused to pull back. Paul repeatedly sent heartfelt messages to others, for he had already devoted himself to building them up and serving them, no matter what the cost.

Moreover, Paul was not concerned about being viewed as soft, weak, or unmanly according to the world's definitions. He knew that the world's definitions of strength and toughness were twisted, just the opposite of God's. In his mind, telling others about their value and specialness would build intimacy, love, and deeper faith for them. Thus, his affirmation of them represented an act of strength, of real mental toughness, not weakness.

By now you may have guessed why I have chosen to deal with this subject. I encourage you to tell those special people in your life how much they mean to you. What about that brother, sister, husband, wife, friend, or parent? Are you willing to give it a try?

Suggested Application. The next time you sense the urge to tell someone that he or she is special to you, try not to choke. Rather, think of one thing that person has done for you in the past. Thank him for that, and then connect your thanks with a statement like: "And that is only one reason why you mean a lot to me."

Here are some examples. A person might say, "Dad, I appreciate the way you have helped me through school all these years. And that is just one reason why you mean a lot to me." Or, "Honey, you have always been so close and supportive. That is just one reason why I think you're special."

Expressing gratitude for specific things will be a natural lead-in to telling people how important they are to you. It will be easier that way. As a result, significant people in your life will be edified and touched.

4

Share the Joy
of Another's Success

Tom serves the high school youth group, and Jack works with the college group in the same church. They are also good friends. At any given moment, they and their wives might get together to bike, play tennis, or have an in-depth conversation over a cup of coffee.

In spite of their apparent closeness, however, Tom is at odds with Jack on a different level. In secret he competes with him over the seeming success of their groups. Tom is preoccupied with the question of which of the two of them is the most esteemed. And his drummed-up criteria for determining the victor is as follows: Who has the largest group? Who is most admired by respective group members? Which group has the most conversions? And which of the two groups is most esteemed by church leaders and members?

With such questions circulating in his mind, Tom draws endless comparisons, giving rise to two general reactions. The first reaction centers on Jack's failures and misfortunes. Whenever Tom senses that Jack's college group does not measure up to his criteria, he cannot help but feel elated. He takes pleasure in seeing even the slightest setback for Jack. And knowing he is able to disguise his gloating, Tom feels no need to change his attitude.

The second reaction centers on any perceived success in Jack's group. Tom takes great displeasure at the slightest hint of it. For example, if Jack's college retreat shows success, Tom erupts with agitation and jealousy. His sense of buoyancy suddenly drops, as gloom sets in. What especially gnaws at him is the thought that Jack's group now might fare better than his in the eyes of others.

Sound familiar? Such self-centered reactions are hardly atypical, since many of us succumb to them, taking twisted pleasure in another's setback or fall. On the other hand, when that perceived competitor succeeds, even in ways that please the Lord, our jealousy swells, bursting into anger.

Surely the Scriptures point to different ways of reacting. When others fall, we are told to empathize and share their burdens. We hope and work for resolution. On the other hand, joy should be shared over another's success when it complies with God's will. Another person's progress need not threaten us; we can delight in it.

Here is a biblical example. Following David's stunning victory over Goliath, King Saul was so captivated by this youth that he brought him into his own household.

Now Saul had a son, Jonathan. And seeing David's grand victory and his father's attentiveness could have deflated him for not shining as bright. Feeling that the spotlight had left him, he could have seethed with bitter jealousy.

But, instead, Jonathan rejoiced in David's success and new-found status. "Jonathan made a covenant with David because he loved him as himself. Jonathan took off the robe he was wearing and gave it to David, along with his tunic, and even his sword, his bow and his belt" (1 Samuel 18:3-4).

At first glance, one might suspect that Jonathan's fine gestures only covered up his real feelings and that underneath was a seething resentment of David, ready to pounce at the right opportunity. However, any suspicion dissolves as the story goes on.

Soon after his entrance into Saul's household, David became increasingly esteemed by the people. His popularity, in turn, made Saul jealous and enraged to the point of plotting to murder him.

Aware of his father's sudden change of heart, Jonathan could have rallied behind his vicious plots. But, instead, fearful of David's impending danger, Jonathan cried out to Saul in David's defense: "Let not the king do wrong to his servant David; he has not wronged you, and what he has done has benefited you greatly" (1 Samuel 19:4).

The fact that Samuel was directed by God to anoint David as

Israel's future king logically spoiled Jonathan's chance to ascend to the throne. And one day, in the heat of a severe argument, Saul reminded him of this. "As long as the son of Jesse lives on this earth, neither you nor your kingdom will be established" (1 Samuel 20:31).

But Jonathan angrily retorted, "Why should he be put to death? What has he done?" (1 Samuel 20:32). Grieved, Jonathan then fled from his father's presence.

Thus, although David's forthcoming enthronement would spell great loss to Jonathan, he was willing to accept it and, I believe, even welcome it. Void of self-centeredness and upright in heart, Jonathan could share David's burdens and the joy of his success.

Surely, Jonathan's reactions are worth emulating. His life offers a challenge to us all.

Suggested Application. When noticing another person—that colleague, friend, or relative—falling in any way, check yourself. Ask yourself: Am I a bit amused or elated by this? In any way am I elevating myself? If "yes" is your answer to either question, confess your reaction as sin to Christ. Then ask Him to help you cultivate a new burden and a new empathy for his or her misfortune.

On the other hand, when noticing another's progress, ask yourself: Am I feeling lower than before, or let down? Does his (or her) success somehow rob me of peace? If your answers indicate a need for change, confess your reactions as sin to Christ. Next, ask Him to help you share both the burdens and the joys of his (or her) success.

In the beginning, such a renewal process might run directly against the grain of your competitive instincts, producing much pain. This will be especially trying as it relates to your arch rival. Nonetheless, persist in striving for change. Eventually, reacting in the right ways will become habitual.

Personally, I have sometimes needed this renewal in my life. And when it has occurred, newfound liberty has replaced a host of problems including bitterness, jealousy, mental revolt, and pride. Moreover, hearing God's voice with an uncluttered mind, I have found myself being led to new places where success, real success, might be mine. God-given success can be one of His ways of affirming my corrected reactions to the failures and successes of others.

5

Handle Relationships with Wisdom

When considering the key message of the book of Job, most people think it is the mystery of suffering and a righteous man's reaction to it. This ancient story offers a striking commentary on how to view and deal with afflictions.

Running parallel to this central theme, though, are several other themes that also embody significant truths. And in this chapter I want to focus on one of them, namely the importance God ascribes to the way we relate and speak to others. He is concerned about whether we employ wisdom in our interaction with them.

As a result of the planning and outpouring of direct satanic attacks, Job lost his servants, camels, donkeys, oxen, and sheep. Worse still were the sudden, tragic deaths of his sons and daughters because of the collapse of the eldest son's house. On top of this, tormenting boils appeared, plaguing Job from head to foot.

Having learned of the calamity, a handful of Job's friends—Eliphaz, Bildad, and Zophar—banded together to visit him, hoping to offer comfort and support. And, upon their meeting, these men were visibly moved by Job's appearance: "And when they lifted up their eyes at a distance, and did not recognize him, they raised their voices and wept. And each of them tore his robe, and they threw dust over their heads toward the sky" (2:12, NASB).

From this point on, though. everything went downhill. The text states that those men sat with Job for seven days and nights without speaking a single word. Certainly, shared silences on such raw occasions are needed and can often do more than a thousand words. But I doubt that their remaining mute for so long was the best policy. For Job was in dire need of comforting words, too.

Finally Job broke the awkward silence with a dismal report of his condition. Eliphaz was the first to respond and set the tone for the subsequent words of advice. And studying Eliphaz's rambling statement reveals that he used no discretion in assessing the reasons for Job's great loss.

For years, Job had been widely known to be an upright, righteous man. At the beginning of his speech, even Eliphaz said, "Think how you have instructed many, how you have strengthened feeble hands. Your words have supported those who stumbled; you have strengthened faltering knees" (Job 4:3-4). Moreover, God declared to Satan: "Have you considered My servant Job? For there is no one like him on the earth, a blameless and upright man, fearing God and turning away from evil" (Job 1:8).

Yet, Eliphaz indicted Job. He was to blame for all of his trouble. "Consider now," he said, "who, being innocent has ever perished? Where were the upright ever destroyed? As I have observed, those who plow evil and those who sow trouble reap it" (Job 4:7-8). Obviously, he was far off the mark!

Sadly, Eliphaz was not the only one who fell into this condemning trap; the others did as well. Committed to their dogmatic, shortsighted statements, they fought to make Job feel guilty. But if he succumbed to it, his would have been false guilt, guilt that God did not want him to have.

Suppose for a moment that Job had agreed with his accusers that his great losses were due to God's judgment for personal sins. Can you see how that reaction might have fulfilled Satan's forecast to God: "Put forth Thy hand, now, and touch his bone and his flesh; he will curse Thee to Thy face" (Job 2:5), thereby fulfilling his evil plot?

If Job had concluded that God's judgment had caused his loss, and then reflected on his own upright heart, he might have concluded that God had overreacted and was, therefore, cruel and harsh in His treatment—not kind and just. Such a conclusion might cause Job to curse God to His face.

Recognizing the possibility of false guilt, Job repudiated their words and maintained his innocence. However, instead of listening, admitting that they did not have all the facts, and giving him the benefit of the doubt, Job's accusers continued to pound away with hard, fast answers. Consequently, those men failed to engage in dialogue—the kind of give-and-take discussion that reveals empathy, sensitivity, and understanding—with Job. Their words incessantly poured out as if Job needed to hear a speech. Can you imagine losing almost everything and then having to face a bunch of ultra-pious sermonizers? It is no small wonder that Job became quite vehement in his own defense!

Examining the content of their speeches, one notices that the theology presented, standing by itself, was not all that bad. In fact, many statements revealed deep theological knowledge. But that knowledge was not used correctly.

Another important ingredient was missing—wisdom. It was not used either to discern the reasons for Job's state or to assess how to meet his needs. Consequently the knowledge was used against him, not for him, thereby compounding his pain.

This should tell us that knowledge, to be relevant, cannot stand alone. It must be coupled with wisdom. I am afraid that too many people within the ranks are like Job's friends, full of theological knowledge but unable to use it.

How did God react to the ill-treatment shown Job? Not lightly, to be sure! This greatly angered Him. Having heard enough, He finally burst out with this statement to Eliphaz: "My wrath is kindled against you and against your two friends, because you have not spoken of Me what is right as My servant Job has" (Job 42:7, NASB).

Seen here, God was keenly aware of the kind of treatment shown Job by his friends. And I firmly believe this holds true for all of our relationships. God is in tune to how we treat and view others. Stated positively, God expects the righteous to exercise wisdom when dealing with others. Books could be written on what this entails. Briefly, exercising wisdom includes accurately assessing where others are emotionally, socially, and spiritually, especially when in distress. It is sensing what they need most.

Then, having made this assessment, words are carefully chosen to meet those needs, to build and encourage those people. But wisdom also tells us when to remain silent, when speaking out would only be counterproductive. Whatever the situation, our actions ought to translate into new life and wholeness in Christ for our friends.

Suggested Application. Ask yourself: Do I resemble Job's friends in any way? Do I need more wisdom when dealing with other people?

If so, here are some suggestions. Ask Christ to enroll you in a life-long course on how to treat others as He did. In response, the Spirit of God will creatively work through varied experiences to help you to gain the needed wisdom.

For example, God might alert you to someone who would model Christlike ways of relating. If that happens, observe how he or she interacts, especially during times of stress. Even with that person, though, be discerning. Since he is human, not everything that he does will reflect God's ways. So soak in the good, but leave out the bad.

Here is another suggestion. Read through the gospel of Luke. As you do, carefully study how Christ employed wisdom when dealing with both the wicked and righteous. Then incorporate what's seen into your own life. As a result, your wise discernment and words will build others up, meet their needs, and shower them with grace (unconditional acceptance), thereby complying with Ephesians 4:29, which reads: "Do not let any unwholesome talk come out of your mouths, but only what is helpful for building others up according to their needs, that it may benefit those who listen."

6
Say Thank You

Beth was bedridden for months with a terminal illness. Finally, recognizing her approaching death, the doctor summoned her four children to her bedside. Feeling drained, but drawing upon their comforting presence, she smiled warmly at them.

After a long silence, her son Joe finally burst out with, "You know, Mom, you've been great to us! You're so special!" No sooner did he complete his sentence than the others reinforced his statement.

"Yeah, Mom, you are so good!"

"How can I tell you how I feel?"

Suddenly, Beth's smile gave way to a grim stare. "Do you kids really mean that?"

"Yes!" they replied in unison.

"Well," she continued, "I wasn't sure you felt that way. You never really said this before. I guess I assumed all along that you weren't that thankful."

How sad! For years, spurred on by sacrificial love, Beth had really "put out" for her children. She had labored cleaning the house, cooking meals, and washing heaps of clothes. Even more important was her readiness to attentively and patiently listen, counsel during times of stress, and engage in loving discipline. Yet, because she never heard it, Beth remained in the dark about their level of gratitude.

Unfortunately, that is hardly an isolated case! More often than not, I have observed people cultivating and exhibiting anything but a thankful attitude toward others. Instead of focusing on the good and on what's right about people, they seem bent on finding the worst in them, then complaining about them. Recently, following our small Bible study/sharing group meeting, my wife, Karen, warmly pointed out to one woman the kindness received from her son who, incidently, was standing nearby.

Instead of responding with joy and congratulating the boy, however, the woman snapped back, "Well, you should just see him at home for one day. Then you wouldn't say that!"

Angered by such insensitive negativism and hoping to cushion the blow for the boy, Karen reemphasized her point. But the woman only held her ground.

Afterward, we discussed the possible long-term repercussions of such a critical, thankless spirit. And the conclusion was drawn that, without change, the boy was a likely candidate for bitterness and rebellion, giving the mother something to really complain about.

Though living in the most affluent and secure nation in history, many people outside and, let me stress, inside the church, act like stubborn children who never cease to take, but cry out in protest at the slightest inconvenience. Someone once called it "the tyranny of spoiled brats."

Such spoiledness is especially widespread among the youth of our country. Year after year they coldly accept everything their parents' work and sacrifice provide without a warm "thanks." And their tyrannical attitude is tolerated even in many Christian homes.

Today's young people are provided with so much materially—in my mind, too much. Yet, all many parents hear is constant grumbling—the bedroom is too small—there are too many chores—restrictions are too limiting and stifling—the neighbor's television set is bigger and has better color—being at home is a drag. I am sure parents who face this know the oppression and the sting of such words. In *King Lear,* William Shakespeare offered this commentary: "How sharper than a serpent's tooth it is to have a thankless child."

On the other hand, isn't it true that in many homes spoiled young people are merely mirroring their parents? They are thankless because their parents are thankless. Thus, for any real change to occur, the parents need to become better models. Through their actions, words, and family traditions, they need to demonstrate the joy of having thankful hearts.

"Thankfully," here and there people can be found who search for the good in others, then express thanks for it. The apostle Paul was that way. Eleven of his thirteen epistles show that gratitude was a natural expression for him.

And Paul expressed his thanks, because he adopted God's perspective. You see, whenever Christ notices the slightest improvement, the slightest growth of righteousness in our lives—such as increased kindness, patience, or love—He is gratified. Moreover, He wants to make His gratitude known to us, in an effort to reinforce such growth. And this is where Paul came in.

Acting as God's messenger, Paul sounded off words of thanksgiving to the deserving, thereby stimulating them to be even more zealous in doing good deeds and pursuing righteousness. For example, to the Roman Christians (Romans 1:8) he said, "I thank my God through Jesus Christ for all of you, because your faith is being reported all over the world." Later on in the same book (16:3-4) he said, "Greet Priscilla and Aquila, my fellow workers in Christ Jesus. They risked their lives for me. Not only I but all the churches of the Gentiles are grateful to them."

Paul was especially touched when he learned of increased love and faith in others. To the Colossian believers (1:3-4), for example, he said, "We always thank God, the Father of our Lord Jesus Christ, when we pray for you, because we have heard of your faith in Christ Jesus and of the love you have for all the saints."

To the Thessalonians he gave these words: "We ought always to thank God for you, brothers, and rightly so, because your faith is growing more and more, and the love every one of you has for each other is increasing" (2 Thessalonians 1:3).

That's a good precedent to follow. Frequently when I'm with others, and especially when I'm counseling, I try to point out any God-inspired deed or Christlike quality of another person. I do this to reinforce what God is working overtime to build into their lives.

As a result, many who otherwise would only fixate on what's wrong about themselves have felt inspired to look at the good that God is placing within them. They come to see that Christ is overhauling and refurbishing their minds, intensifying their drive to be the persons God wants them to be.

Not only are people encouraged and touched upon receiving words of gratitude, but Christ is also touched when He receives them. He esteems genuine expressions of gratitude for the gifts He has given. Moreover, He is free to give more.

Imagine that you have purchased two gifts for a nephew for Christmas. On Christmas day, you bring one gift into his home and leave the other one, meant to be a last-minute surprise, out in the car.

Come gift-giving time, your nephew rips through your present's wrappings with abandon, expecting the best. But, opening the box, his face suddenly drops.

"Thanks, uh, you shouldn't have done it," he says, without any indication of real gratitude. "Let's see what else is under the tree."

How would you feel? Such a thankless response would tell me to leave the other gift in the car and then give it to another person or to him another day. If not, the selfish attitude he showed for the first gift would probably be displayed toward the second one as well, spoiling its intended value and reinforcing his self-centeredness.

Christ does the same with us. Certain gifts are given by Him while others are kept out of sight. Then He observes our reactions to the ones we have received.

If our responses resemble that nephew's, Christ may keep some of His other gifts, sometimes His best ones, out of sight until we show real gratitude for the ones already received. For, if given, they too would receive thankless responses, spoiling their intended value and reinforcing our self-centeredness.

On the other hand, if we are full of gratitude upon receiving God's gifts, and then quick to express it, He feels appreciated. Christ's heart is warmed. Seeing that our responses draw out the desired value of His gifts as well as the best in us, He feels free to give us more and sometimes even shock us with the unexpected. God takes pleasure in giving to those with grateful hearts.

A thankful heart draws out the best in us for several reasons. People who are thankless are usually stewing about something. Their minds are constantly fixed upon what they want. And the ensuing mental agitation causes bitterness, sometimes leading to depression. Because such a person is never content, his mind is always in a state of conflict, producing mental stress (see Romans 1:21).

A grateful heart, however, does just the opposite. It helps to shape a mindset of acceptance, contentment, and peace. Because a thankful heart protects a person from being consumed by the pains and setbacks of this world, that person is better equipped to endure them. A thankful heart enables him to "endure all things" (1 Corinthians 13:7), while it builds a healthy, positive mind.

Every good thing finds its source in God: friends, food, health, jobs, mountains, the ocean—everything. James 1:17 reads: "Every good and perfect gift is from above, coming down from the Father of the heavenly lights, who does not change like shifting shadows."

God is the supreme giver! And the thing that He desires to give most of all is Himself. Christ's friendship and unconditional love are the ultimate gifts, the ones our hearts long for until found.

Suggested Application. If you need to, set a new precedent for yourself: make special efforts to say, "Thanks." Periodically, upon meeting special people in your life, think of one deed or quality for which you are especially grateful, then express it to them.

Try to include your children, mother, father, spouse, special friends, employer, employee, and others. For example, when conversing with your parents, you might say, "Mom and Dad, you have always asked me how things were going in school and at work. Thank you for all of those questions; they showed real concern and love."

The same might be said to one's wife: "You know, dear, it just occurred to me that whenever I'm away from home, I never have to worry about the children. I know you will always give them your best. I don't want to take this for granted any longer. Thanks for doing such a good job with the kids. Thanks for being you!"

Along with conveying such messages in person, use letters and phone calls. Whatever medium you use, giving thanks just might provide the encouragement your loved ones need most.

Be sure to offer words of thanks to Christ, to whom we should be especially grateful. Be like the psalmists. Periodically throughout the day, thank God for His abounding gifts, especially the gift of His unconditional love and friendship. In response, He will feel appreciated, as opposed to being taken for granted. Christ's heart will be warmed.

7

Repay Your Offenders with Kindness

Picture in your mind two youngsters playing marbles, both of them grimly determined to win. Everything is going fine until John notices that Pete is the near victor. Panic-stricken at the prospect of losing his esteemed catseye collection, John desperately waves his arm back and forth through the marbles scattering them in every direction.

Shocked and angered, Pete quickly gathers his belongings and snarls, "John, I have never liked you anyway! I'll never play with you again—never!"

If you are a parent, more than likely you are familiar with this pattern. It may even be a daily ritual in your home. Hurt and enraged by a brother or sister, your child retaliates. And this counterattack may take the form of hitting, name-calling, screaming, or whatever will even the score.

"Well, kids will be kids!" we say to ourselves. But wait a minute: Are children the only ones who play this attack/counter-attack game? No. Adults play it, too. In fact, many adults are more skilled and deadly at this than any child could be. They have spent years beefing up their weaponry. They are experts at going straight for the jugular.

More than likely you can come up with names of people belonging to this camp, people like Neil and his wife, Carol. Normally in private the two get along well. However, in public, they clash while competing to be the most magnetic, the most well-liked.

One evening while having dinner with several other couples, Carol was telling a story. Neil picked up an error in her explanation. Quickly seizing upon the opportunity to look better, he rudely interrupted. "Oh, Carol, you *never* get the facts straight! I sometimes wonder why you even try. Here is how the story goes—"

A week later Neil and Carol happened to be with the same couples when someone began subtly mocking some of his unprofitable business practices. Recalling her prior humiliation, Carol jumped into the conversation with: "You know, you're right! Sometimes Neil is kind of dumb at making business decisions. But take my advice. Don't try to get him to change. He won't listen to you, anyway!"

Score: One for Neil. One for Carol. Zero for the marriage. A good counter-puncher, Carol was able to get even. However, although this brought on a twisted sense of satisfaction, she merely degraded herself and wounded the marriage by returning evil for evil. Also, by playing Neil's game, she allowed herself to be controlled by him.

"Controlled by him, how?" you might ask. The truth is, whenever we react with revenge toward someone who offends us, we are being controlled by him. We are lowering ourselves to play his game. If someone harshly criticizes me and I harshly criticize back, he hooks me into acting just like him. Therefore he "puppets" me.

In line with this principle, instead of maintaining self-control, Carol belittled her husband as he had her. Therefore, she was being controlled. Instead of Carol's pulling her own strings, Neil was pulling them.

Keenly aware of the vindictive nature of man, the apostle Paul exhorted the Roman Christians: "Do not repay anyone evil for evil" (Romans 12:17). To another church, he said, "Make sure that nobody pays back wrong for wrong, but always try to be kind to each other and to everyone else" (1 Thessalonians 5:15).

Touching on the same theme, Peter stressed: "Do not repay evil with evil or insult with insult, but with blessing . . . " (1 Peter 3:9).

Repay with a blessing. Not too easy, is it? Sometimes it even seems impossible. Nevertheless, in no uncertain terms, that is what we are told to do.

Often when hurt by another, the temptation comes: "Do

yourself a favor. Even the score! You owe it to yourself." No matter how justified this reaction might seem, though, succumbing to it is hazardous. Vengeance never serves anyone's good. Others are harmed, and so are we.

Every time we are sucked into returning evil for evil, we lose ground, emotionally and spiritually. We become less than what we were before. On the other hand, returning good for evil brings out the best in us. The benefits are many. We remain free from degrading instincts, free to be more complete persons. We find new joy and vitality for living and gain a greater ability to hear God's voice. And our self-respect grows as we find our thoughts and reactions becoming like Christ's.

Here is a biblical illustration that clarifies what I mean. As you recall, driven by jealous hatred of David's growing popularity, Saul stalked him to murder him. Accompanied by 3,000 choice men, Saul came one day to a cave and entered it. But, although he did not know it, David and his friends happened to be hiding there in that same cave.

Recognizing this to be the perfect opportunity for revenge, David's aides urged him to murder Saul. However, he refused to comply. Minutes later, Saul left the cave. Next, after walking a certain distance from it, he was stunned by a booming voice coming from behind him. "My lord the King!" (1 Samuel 24:8).

Turning sharply around, he saw David near the cave's mouth, lying down with his face to the ground. He continued, "This day you have seen with your own eyes how the LORD delivered you into my hands in the cave. Some urged me to kill you, but I spared you; I said, 'I will not lift my hand against my master, because he is the Lord's anointed!'" (1 Samuel 24:10).

Humiliated by the obvious contrasting qualities of life, Saul then wept with a loud voice.

Seen here, David had the perfect opportunity to repay Saul for all the misery he received, to return evil for evil. However, he was not going to lower himself to Saul's level. He was not about to let a mad king hook him into degrading himself. Instead, seeing Saul's vulnerability, David took the opportunity to be kind and merciful. He repaid Saul with a blessing.

It is unfortunate that Carol, the woman mentioned earlier, did not follow that principle. Suppose that, after being humiliated by her husband, she had decided against getting even when someone mocked his business practices. Instead of saying, "Neil is kind of dumb at making business decisions," she might have said, "Well, perhaps Neil hasn't always made the best choices. But he has made a lot of good ones, too. He tries his best. I can always count on that."

Certainly, Carol would have shown herself to be free, as opposed to being conditioned by human instincts and other people. Along with this, the chances for a change in Neil would have been greater. Surprised by and grateful for Carol's gracious spirit, he might have committed himself to change. "You could have easily evened the score just now for how I humiliated you last week. But, you didn't. Will you forgive me?"

Herein lies the beauty of giving a blessing instead. It can crush the vicious circle of endless attacks and counter-attacks, bringing healing and warmth to relationships.

Suggested Application. With Christ as our prime example, evildoers must be shown goodness instead of revenge. Certainly, the need could arise to verbally defend oneself, as Christ sometimes did with those who opposed Him. Throughout the Bible, righteous men are seen offering legitimate defenses. God could lead you to do the same. However, retaliative measures need not be a part of your defense.

If there is a real desire on your part to give a blessing instead, some interesting developments might occur. As God changed circumstances to bring King Saul to a vulnerable place before David, He might do the same with that evildoer troubling you. At that point, if you were willing, you could easily draw blood. You will know it, and so will he.

But then take that opportunity to be kind and merciful. Repay with goodness. Then watch the results. It is quite possible that your opponent will melt with humiliation, admit his error, and ask for your forgiveness. Regardless of his reaction, though, realize that in a new and refreshing way you have become more like Christ.

8
Be Patient

Ruth and Joe were driving home from a social gathering. A cold silence permeated the car until she broke the ice with: "What's wrong with you?"

"Well," he responded, "like usual, you just weren't with it tonight! Everyone was having a good time, but you couldn't have spoken to more than two people."

"But you know how shy I am with others," Ruth retorted. "You know how insecure and intimidated I feel in groups. I'm trying to improve, though. I spoke with four different people tonight. That's progress!"

"Maybe!" Joe added in a harsh tone, "but you still have a long way to go! I just wish you'd get over this shyness thing, once and for all!"

Ruth bent over, laid her face in her hands, and wept. "From now on you can go by yourself. Why should I even try? All you do is criticize me, anyway!"

Besides being harsh and insensitive, what word best describes Joe? Impatient. Rather than patiently waiting for Ruth to mature gradually, he demanded instant change. There was no openness to the needed process of growth that sometimes requires years.

Also, Joe ignored the constructive use of reinforcement. Focusing on and showing joy for the growth that had already occurred would have given Ruth added incentive to strive for change. But, instead, crushed by Joe's brutal words, she felt like giving up altogether. Further withdrawal seemed like the only way out, since nothing seemed to satisfy him, anyway. Thus, although Joe's hardness was meant to spur on change, it proved to be counterproductive. His rough manner forced the steam out of her, the steam needed for change. Impatience has a way of doing that.

Due, in part, to the fact that exhibiting patience stimulates others to grow, the Scriptures repeatedly stress the need for it. For example, Paul stated, "We urge you, brethren, admonish the unruly, encourage the fainthearted, help the weak, be patient with all men" (1 Thessalonians 5:14, NASB). Notice the inclusive "all men." Patience should not be withheld from anyone.

"Yes, but sometimes I'm afraid that patience is the same as indifference and resignation," someone says. "I'll patiently stand by while others make a mess of their lives." Be assured that when we're required and directed by Christ to do so, we can correct. But the correction must be coupled with showing patience. The two are not incompatable. In fact, with the proper balance, they reinforce each other.

Think again of Paul's words. Notice that just prior to stating, "Be patient with all men," he said. "Admonish the unruly." That means that suggestions and sometimes warnings should be issued to those living disorderly, undisciplined lives. We must not stand idly by while they self-destruct. But, again, constructive criticism should be offered with a spirit of patience.

In the described text, the Greek word used for patience was *makrothumeo*, meaning "to be patient." And it interests me that its Greek counterpart is *oxuthumeo*, which means "to be short-tempered." Thus, the mechanics of these words seems to indicate that a person feels either patience or short-temperedness; they are mutually exclusive. Relationships like Joe and Ruth's testify to this truth. Instead of being patient, he was short-tempered. And, as shown earlier, his short-tempered response only triggered further complications in her, giving him more reasons to be angry.

Ruth undoubtedly would have fared far better if lovingkindness and patience had been shown to her instead. Think of what this statement might have meant: "Ruth, tonight I noticed that you were talking to different people. Good! Think of the progress that's been made. Keep up the good work, OK? I have faith in you."

Patience therefore must be shown to others, especially those closest to us. Then we can sit back, cheer them on, and watch them grow!

Suggested Application. In case you have identified a personal need for more patience, let me ask: Are you patient with yourself? Do you tend to get easily down on and short-tempered with yourself, especially when you make mistakes?

These are key questions. You see, we tend to treat and view others the way we treat and view ourselves. Thus, if I am impatient with you, it more than likely shows that I am impatient with myself. This is not a hard and fast rule, but a general tendency.

In light of this principle, one important step toward renewal is: You need to learn to be more patient with yourself. Patience must be directed inward. Then it will be more natural to be patient with others.

To serve this end, I recommend that you look to God. Christ is patient, even when we fail. This does not mean He does not want growth, for He does. And sometimes God's discipline hurts. But, through it all, He is patient. In 1 Corinthians 13:4, Paul said, "Love is patient." And in 1 John 4:16, we see that "God is love." Now since love is patient and God is love, God is patient. He is patient with you. And since God is patient with you, you can be patient with yourself.

With this conclusion in mind, I suggest the following mental exercise. Whenever you fail, work toward change. But, in the meantime, remind yourself: "Christ is patient with me. Therefore I can be patient with myself." And, as you learn to be patient with yourself, you will find that you have increased patience for others.

9
Listen As Christ Would

Can you recall an incident in which you were trying to express a certain feeling or drive home a certain point, but your listener was not exactly with you? Instead, he or she seemed preoccupied with himself. To make matters worse, you got the distinct impression that you had better hurry up and spit out what was on your mind, for he would soon speak up.

Perhaps you come up with several names. For, speaking bluntly, there are very few good listeners around. Most people are much more prepared to talk than to listen.

Yes, people do converse. Countless words are spoken. Yet, how many are truly absorbed in what is being said? Too often, people are mentally fixed on what they intend to say next. And that is usually caused by an obsession about how they come across, with their own social images.

You see, in their minds listening just doesn't draw the same attention and esteem from others that speaking does. It makes less of a statement and is therefore less important, sometimes even a sign of weakness. After all, don't strong personalities control others with the power of their words? Their discussions are therefore the dialogue of the deaf!

As seen in Matthew 22:34-40, Christ stressed that loving God with all one's heart is most important, and loving others is second on the list. Now if I truly love someone, I will have an absorbing interest in him. I will have a drive to understand intents and feelings behind his words. And compelled by that drive, I will eagerly listen to him. The fact that many Christians are poor listeners tells me that they are clearly failing with the second most important task given us. Unwilling to shake loose from their self-centered tendency toward monologue, they too, along with unbelievers, contribute to the dialogue of the deaf.

Christ was different, wasn't He? Here was a Man who was given the most important mission in history. Yet, Jesus repeatedly took time to listen intently and patiently to individuals, even when passing through suffocating crowds. He was never too busy to stop and listen.

A fascinating illustration of that is seen in Christ's postresurrection encounter with two disciples on their way to Emmaus (Luke 24:13-33). Sensitive to their great distress at the shocking finality of His death, Jesus approached and spoke with these two, keeping His identity hidden. And studying their interaction, it becomes clear that He was an excellent listener.

Christ asked these men,

"What are you discussing together as you walk along?"

They stood still, their faces downcast. One of them, named Cleopas, asked him, "Are you the only one living in Jerusalem who doesn't know the things that have happened there in these days?"

"What things?" He asked.

"About Jesus of Nazareth," they replied. "He was a prophet, powerful in word and deed before God and all the people." (Luke 24:17-19)

Then the two went on to give a fuller explanation of the crucifixion and the events that followed it.

As the three approached Emmaus, Jesus acted as if He would go no farther. But His two companions urged Him to remain with them, and He consented. Having arrived at the village, they sat down to eat, and Christ began breaking bread. Then, as they finally recognized Him, He vanished from their sight.

Notice that Christ was not preoccupied with Himself. He had just experienced barbaric torture on the cross and was freshly risen from the grave. Nevertheless, He was truly absorbed in what the two others felt and had to say.

Christ also asked probing questions that required in-depth

responses. He was not interested in surface comments. Rather, His questions were meant to draw out what was stirring inside of these two people.

Then having asked probing questions, Christ patiently took the time to hear out both of them. He gave them ample room to reflect and to speak. Unlike many of us, Jesus did not pound away with the nonverbal message "Hurry up and spit out what's on your mind!"

And let me stress: Christ listens to each one of us with the same intensity of concern and sensitivity.

Approaching Emmaus, Christ was asked to accompany them farther. Here He had tons of things on His mind. Yet, He consented as if to say, "I'm willing to give you even more of my time, to talk, and yes, to listen."

Suggested Application. Are your listening skills like Christ's? If not, I encourage you to sharpen them.

Here are three concrete suggestions, based on Christ's example. First, become genuinely interested in others. Do not be preoccupied with how you come across, or with your social image. Rather, go beyond yourself and become truly absorbed in what others feel and think. Determine to end any tendency toward self-centered monologue.

Second, develop the art of asking probing questions. Ask creative questions that take you beyond the obvious, revealing deep insights and thereby deepening your understanding.

Third, while asking probing questions, let your partner know that he is not being rushed. You do not keep a stopwatch. He must be given ample room both to reflect and to speak.

Certainly, circumstances do not always permit us to listen at the moment. For example, when the man of the house is rushing off to work, he may not have time to listen to his questioning daughter. But he should indicate to her that sufficient time will be provided later.

I also encourage you to plunge into a small Bible study/prayer and sharing group, if you have not done so already. There, you will be stimulated to really tune into others and probe with good questions. The listening skills gained can then be applied to other relationships.

As a result, your listening skills will sharpen, leading to more penetrating understanding of people. This discipline will help you to develop your listening skills into a ministry, deeply touching the lives of others.

10
Reach Out and Touch

Can you think of one instance in the Bible when an angel touched a person? "That's easy," someone says, "what about the angel who wrestled Jacob until dawn? He touched his thigh in order to dislocate it." Yes, that's one example. But perhaps you are unaware of other cases where angels touched people for reasons other than discipline. Several times, their touch provided a tangible way to comfort, encourage, and strengthen.

Let me illustrate. As described in 1 Kings 19, Elijah, panic-stricken at the prospect of being slain by the wicked queen, Jezebel, ran for miles until falling in exhaustion near a broom tree. There, he fell asleep but later was awakened by the touch of an angel, who said, "Get up and eat" (v. 5).

Here, I do not believe that the angel touched Elijah merely to awaken him. Shouting, "Wake up!" would have sufficed for that purpose. Rather, like a mother touching her sleeping child in the morning, the angel intended also to support and strengthen Elijah.

Another example is seen in the life of Daniel. The angel Gabriel was sent to give him understanding of a certain vision. But, upon Gabriel's arrival, Daniel melted with paralyzing fear. Falling on his face, Daniel sank into a deep sleep, only to be revived by the angel's gentle touch, raising him to his feet (see Daniel 8:15-18).

Here again, as with Elijah, the angel's touch was not only

meant to awaken Daniel but also to comfort and support him. What beautiful expressions of compassion the angel's touch conveyed to those nerve-wrecked men!

Such expressions are especially significant when we consider that they mirror what was true about our Lord. Examining the gospels, we notice that Christ did the same thing repeatedly. As an intimate, tangible expression of His compassion for them, He was constantly touching His contemporaries.

A fascinating example of this occurred during Christ's transfiguration. Having brought Peter, James, and John to the top of a high mountain, Jesus became transfigured before them. A bright cloud then overshadowed them, out of which God spoke, saying, "This is my Son, whom I love; with him I am well pleased. Listen to him!" (Matthew 17:5).

Terrified, the three disciples fell with their faces to the ground. But the Lord had compassion on them. The story continues: "But Jesus came and touched them. 'Get up,' he said. 'Don't be afraid'" (Matthew 17:7).

Though the three men were frozen with fear, that must have been a very special moment for them. Being touched by Christ after catching a glimpse of His glorified state was exhilarating. And I believe that was just one of many times He touched the disciples. John evidently felt comfortable leaning against Him during the Last Supper.

Certainly, Jesus did not reserve this expression only for the Twelve. Literally hundreds felt His hand during His three-year ministry. Christ readily laid His hands on the blind, lame, lepers, and others who needed healing. For example, once He heard two blind men crying out for mercy. "And moved with compassion, Jesus touched their eyes; and immediately they regained their sight, and followed Him" (Matthew 20:34, NASB). The gospels are filled with such reports.

Touching the sick, however, was not necessary for the cure itself to occur. As Jesus demonstrated through the healing of the centurion's servant, He needed only to give "the word." His touch was meant, then, in large measure, to convey loving concern, to personalize the act, and to add meaning to the healing event.

Since touch played such a key role in Christ's service and in that of the angels, it can play an important part in ours as well. A firm hand on someone's shoulder, an arm around the back, a hand around the back of the neck, a warm embrace—all of these, given at the right time and place, can communicate a powerful message.

In fact, sometimes touch does more than a thousand words to provide what's needed.

I say "at the right time and place" because, though a potentially useful tool, touch can also be abused, causing great harm to both parties involved. I am thinking particularly of some pastors who have foolishly crossed certain boundaries with women. A touch of the hand or a friendly embrace, though innocent at first, has sometimes aroused an interest to add sexual overtones to subsequent contacts, leading sometimes to sexual involvement. A number of ministers have fallen that way.

Because of the physical context of the Christian counselor's work—namely, the one-to-one relationship behind closed doors—he must be especially cautious. As part of their graduate training, many counseling students are taught that touch can act as a catalyst for therapy. However, a number of them, having bought that idea, have stumbled.

Although sexual involvement might not be the end-product of touch in such a setting, other dangers exist. For example, it could be misread by either party as a sign of romantic love, giving rise to unhealthy fantasies. That is especially apt to occur if a person is insecure and starved for affection.

Because of these dangers and others, I highly recommend that counselors and pastors refrain from touching women during private counseling, regardless of the problems presented. If a woman is distressed, she can be consoled with comforting words, Scripture reading, and prayer. That standard may sound rigid. But too many dangers exist for both parties for the wise counselor to do otherwise. I have learned of too many casualities, even among strong believers.

Leaving the counseling scene, I contend that men and women within the Body of Christ can touch each other, but usually within group contexts. Whether touching men or women, when compelled by loving, pure motives, touch can become a powerful instrument in Christ's hands to comfort, edify, and deepen relationships.

Suggested Application. Like Christ and the angels, are you making good use of touch? Has this tool become part of your personal ministry? If not, I encourage you to dare to use it. Of course, you will need to exercise sensitivity with respect to timing, place, and purpose. But do not be restrained or rigid about using it.

For example, when another person feels defeated, an arm

placed around his back can do much to bring relief. When someone suffers with a crushing loss, a firm hand on the shoulder or a warm embrace might do more than a thousand words to console and support him.

Touch can also send wholesome messages during less serious times. A pat on the back or a soft punch to the arm can convey special feelings of care, interest, and liking. Such physical expressions can enhance mutual love and trust.

So, in short, compelled by pure, loving motives, dare to touch others. People and relationships will be healed in the process.

11

Confront with Care

Imagine for a moment that you serve the youth group in your church. If you do already, this shouldn't require much energy on your part. For several years you have diligently worked, counseled youth and parents, prepared well for weekly meetings, and held many good retreats. You have gone well past the call of duty.

One day, a church elder gives you the name of a new family in town in which are two youth who have expressed interest in joining your group.

"Please contact this family right away," he says. "I've known these kids for years. They'd fit well in your group."

"I'll get on it right away," you respond. But you don't. With tons of things weighing on your mind, you procrastinate and forget to make the contact.

Weeks pass. One day as you're going out of the church, this elder walks briskly up to you and shouts, "What's wrong with you?!"

"What do you mean?"

"What I mean is that you didn't make contact with that new family! You said you would, but you didn't! Man, you really blew it on this one!"

If this happened to you, how would you feel? Would his words encourage you to be more conscientious at making contacts in the future? Perhaps. It is to be hoped that you could take his advice without becoming embittered in return. However, the natural reaction would be one of anger and dismay. Mental revolt. I would probably think: *Yes, I blew it. I've got to do better. But he spoke as if I couldn't do anything right! He acted as if I had no concern for youth, even though I've worked with them for years!*

Obviously, such a short-sighted approach would be more harmful than constructive. More than likely, it would backfire.

"Are you saying we should avoid confronting others?" someone might ask.

No. In fact, I contend that we do not confront enough, in love, within the Body of Christ. Because of apathy, indifference, and self-centeredness, we have a strong tendency to let other people go on their merry own way, falling into the same traps over and over again. Too many people within the church stand idly by as others self-destruct.

We need to confront when it is required. But how this is done is all-important. If our words belittle and crush, or if we focus on the bad in a way that conveys there is no good, our listeners might only see red.

Hoping to shield their own self-esteem, they may deafen their ears to our voices. The issue becomes: "How can I protect myself? How can I get this guy off my back?" not, "How can I improve?"

There exists a constructive way to confront without pushing our listeners into a stance of self-defense. How? By presenting the total picture.

Let me explain what I mean by going to the Scriptures. As we can see at the beginning of the book of Revelation, Christ saw fit to correct several churches. Confrontation was required, since they were falling short in certain disciplines.

Addressing the church in Ephesus, Christ said:

> I know your deeds, your hard work and your perseverance. I know that you cannot tolerate wicked men, that you have tested those who claim to be apostles but are not, and have found them false. You have persevered and have endured hardships for my name, and have not grown weary. Yet I hold this against you: You have forsaken your first love. Remember the height from which you have fallen! Repent and do the things you did at first. (Revelation 2:2-5)

Notice Christ's approach. He began by focusing on the good—the Ephesians' hard work, perseverance, and wise testing of the apostles. First, He affirmed them for what they were doing right. Then having assured them, Christ turned to their need for change. "You have forsaken your first love. Remember the height from which you have fallen!" (vv. 4-5).

Seen here, Jesus did not use sugar-coated words. Rather, He was blunt in sending "reality messages." Yet, I believe that the Ephesians reacted favorably. Surely, hearing from God had something to do with it. But, His positive approach made a difference, too. By the time Christ came to correcting them, the Ephesians already felt affirmed and encouraged for what they had been doing right. And along with God's love and grace, that supplied the motivation and energy for change.

Think what might have happened if Christ had focused only on the negative. The Ephesians could have painfully questioned whether the Lord even recognized their good deeds. Then, wondering if their past efforts ever counted, they might have given up in despair. But since Christ presented the total picture, the good with the bad, the Ephesians knew that what they had done in His name really did matter.

Christ used the same approach with several other churches, in the second and third chapters of Revelation. To the church in Thyatira, He began by stressing the positive: "I know your deeds, your love and faith, your service and perseverance, and that you are now doing more than you did at first" (Revelation 2:19).

Then having affirmed them, Christ confronted them: "Nevertheless, I have this against you: You tolerate that woman Jezebel, who calls herself a prophetess. By her teaching she misleads my servants into sexual immorality and the eating of food sacrificed to idols" (Revelation 2:20). Again, Jesus presented the total picture, showing Himself to be both just and sensitive.

"This looks like a good approach," someone might say, "but must I present the total picture every time I confront?"

Surely, time and circumstances do not always allow us to present the good first, especially within the context of one's family or job. But if we are quick to reinforce what's right, if we make special efforts to affirm when due, then the positive and negative need not be coupled back to back. Time gaps can occur between the two.

Using the described method should be particularly considered, though, when the wayward person is apt to misread the criticism because of being overly sensitive or when his confronter is driving home an earth-shaking point.

Think again of the elder mentioned earlier. Using Christ's approach, he would have been wiser to say: "You know, I really appreciate the work you've been doing with the young people.

Your counseling and teaching have meant a lot to them and their parents. But I need to point out a weakness, too. Do you remember the new family I mentioned several weeks ago? You did not make the contact with them as you had agreed to. Be sure to contact them, would you? And I think you could be more prompt at making contacts, OK?"

I can surely vouch for the effectiveness of presenting the total picture. I use it regularly in my counseling and everyday relationships. And most people, even those in trouble with the law, have responded favorably to this positive approach. Feeling affirmed and supported supplies the motivation and energy to change.

Suggested Application. Carefully read the second and third chapters of the book of Revelation. Closely study Christ's confronting approach with the churches. Then practice what you have observed with those around you.

When a need arises to correct someone, prior to the actual encounter think of something good and positive about that person. Do not select a physical characteristic, such as good looks, but rather acts of love and wholesome Christlike qualities.

Next, pray for words of wisdom, along with the right reaction to your words. Upon meeting that person, without appearing condescending, begin by expressing the good. Having affirmed him, proceed with firmness—but also with gentleness and love—to point out the area in need of change. Encourage growth. Then relax, knowing that like Christ you have presented the total picture.

12

Watch God Mirror Your Weaknesses Through Others

Can you think of two people in the same biblical story who were renowned deceivers? Tricksters? Jacob and his uncle Laban come to my mind.

Certainly, Jacob was a master schemer. Consider, for example, how he deceived his own father, Isaac. As depicted in Genesis chapter 27, as he died, Isaac planned to give Esau, his oldest son, what was due him: the final blessing.

Realizing this, Jacob schemed with his mother, Rebekah, so that he would receive it instead. Taking advantage of Isaac's poor vision, he put on Esau's garments and placed goatskins on his hands and neck, for Esau was a hairy man.

Then Jacob approached his father, who asked, "Who is it?" (v. 18).

"I am Esau, your firstborn" (v. 19).

Yet, that did not satisfy Isaac. Confused, he said, "Come near so I can touch you, my son, to know whether you really are my son Esau or not" (v. 21).

Touching Jacob, he added, "The voice is the voice of Jacob, but the hands are the hands of Esau" (v. 22).

Still confused, he asked again. "Are you really my son Esau?" (v. 24).

"I am," Jacob replied (v. 24). So Isaac proceeded to bless him, thinking he was Esau and being fooled by his own son. If you were to read the entire story of Jacob, his trickery would become evident on several other occasions as well.

Having discussed Jacob, let's look at the second schemer, Laban. After learning of Jacob's deception of Isaac, Esau vowed to murder him. Terror-stricken, Jacob then fled to his uncle Laban's home in Haran.

Sometime after their meeting, Jacob made a covenant with Laban to serve him for seven years in exchange for his daughter Rachel's hand in marriage (Genesis 29:18).

When the seven years had been completed, Jacob reminded Laban of their prior agreement. A wedding feast was then celebrated. But later that evening, Laban tricked him by giving him his older daughter, Leah, instead of Rachel.

Assuming she was Rachel, Jacob lay with her, only to discover the next morning that he had been wronged. Stirred with wrath, he approached Laban, crying out: "What is this you have done to me? I served you for Rachel, didn't I? Why have you deceived me?" (Genesis 29:25). A reflection of what happened to Esau, wasn't it?

But that was not the last time Jacob was deceived. Laban continued to draw from his bag of nasty tricks. Jacob was forced to work another full seven years for Rachel (vv. 27-30). On top of that, his wages were changed ten times.

Herein, one schemer is seen contending with another. But I do not believe that their meeting was merely coincidental. It was planned by God from the start.

God knew all too well that Jacob's deceptive nature would have to be rooted out before he could become the faithful person, the spiritual leader, and the patriarch he was meant to be. Without a change, Jacob's cunning would repeatedly disrupt God's plan for his life, not to mention the fate of the forthcoming state of Israel.

Thus, God was eager to get Jacob to see his dire need for change. And for this purpose and others, He sent Jacob to live with Laban. God could get Jacob to see himself more clearly through his uncle. Suffering the consequences of Laban's schemings would encourage him to identify, be repulsed by, and then pluck out the same problem within himself.

This story fascinates me, because God sometimes does the same thing with us. Wanting to alert us to some need for change, He brings another person into our lives who bears a similar problem and mirrors ours.

It is to be hoped that, when this occurs, we are receptive to God's voice, shouting, "You need to work on this, too!" We should confess, if needed, and cooperate with Him so that the change is realized.

If we are reluctant to listen and cooperate, however, God might allow the other person's flaw to really sting us so that we become repulsed by the sight of it, within ourselves as well. Again, that is what happened to Jacob.

Some time ago, I met a person named Bob, who had a terrible habit of criticizing other people. He was quick to belittle even his close friends. And for quite a while, he saw no need for change.

The day came when a position needed to be filled in Bob's office. And the replacement for this vacancy had a problem with—you guessed it—criticizing others.

Recognizing the condemning nature of this man, Bob heard God's voice shouting through his pains: "You have the same problem." However, he was slow to change. So to speed things up, God allowed Bob to be stung repeatedly, which, in turn, led to a repulsion toward this trait, along with a drive to eliminate it within himself.

I have especially seen God use this process to mirror over-competitiveness with others. For example, Joan was raised in a home filled with sibling rivalry. Her background, though Christian, created such a competitive spirit within her that she saw other people as objects to outdo rather than as persons to love.

Noticing this, God gave Joan a new roommate, who possessed the same flaw. And soon, these women found themselves combating to outflank the other for popularity, success at work, and other visible achievements. The day finally came, though, when Joan began to read God's writing on the wall. *It is not coincidental that she is so competitive like me,* she realized. *Maybe God is telling me something.*

Unfortunately, many believers fail to profit from this mirroring process. Why? Some are so busy justifying themselves that they fail to see God working this way. Others clearly recognize His proddings but pridefully resist change, stubbornly clutching their flaws.

We must be different, because openness to Christ's reflecting process greatly enhances emotional and spiritual growth. Once we realize the lesson God has for us, we will not need to bear the same pain repeatedly. Cooperating with God will serve His purpose in the mirroring process. Most important, if we are open to His purpose, we stand a better chance of bearing the striking image of Christ, instead of the image of a negative trait.

Suggested Application. Be open and sensitive to God's mirroring process. Upon noticing a flaw in another person, take a quick inventory of yourself, especially if the trait repeats itself. Maybe Christ is lovingly telling you something.

Let me, however, sound a warning. Be careful not to think that every person crossing your path is meant to reflect a personal problem. Doing so could lead to morbid introspection, preoccupation with self, and a fear of meeting new people.

Upon hearing God's voice saying, "You have the same problem," immediately confess it and ask Christ for the ability and power to get rid of it. Take full advantage of the means God lays in your path for change.

This might mean sharing your problem with one or more trusted friends who could offer wise, practical counsel. In-depth counseling might be required with a sound Christian counselor or pastor. It is even possible that Christ would direct you to share your discovery with the person who acts as your mirror, and then invite him or her to work on the same problem together.

13

Escape the
Jealousy Trap

"The night is almost gone, and the day is at hand. Let us therefore lay aside the deeds of darkness and put on the armor of light. Let us behave properly as in the day, not in carousing and drunkenness, not in sexual promiscuity and sensuality, not in strife and jealousy" (Romans 13:12-13, NASB).

What the apostle Paul wrote in that passage to the Roman Christians gives just a sample of what darkens the mind. And, in this chapter, I want to focus on the last item mentioned, jealousy.

If a survey were taken to discover the number of believers that commit the sins listed by Paul, relatively few would answer "yes" to carousing, drunkenness, and sexual promiscuity. But that would not be the case with jealousy.

That green-eyed monster thrives not only in the secular world but also in many Christian families and churches. In fact, some of the most jealous people I have known were believers.

When jealousy shows its ugly head, normally coupled with it is a strange sense of justice. People feel right about it and expect to gain from it. However, jealousy can bring only loss. It has a decaying effect upon minds and relationships. That is why the Scriptures command us to discard it like garbage.

Why is jealousy so lethal? Have you ever noticed how it forces us to be obsessed with its object? Like metal to a powerful magnet, our attention is constantly drawn to whatever or whoever provoked the jealousy. As a result, our vision narrows. Our field of consciousness is constricted. In the meantime, because the mind can entertain only one thought at a time, reflections of a positive or wholesome nature are tossed out. Our thought life becomes negatively charged.

Moreover, as the mind becomes fixated on the object of jealousy, angry feelings are unleashed, forcing us to fixate even more, thereby provoking even deeper feelings of jealousy. Can you see how the whole process becomes a vicious circle?

Caught in this vicious circle, our minds become increasingly irrational and bitter-toned. Think back to a time when you were jealous of someone. When jealousy reigned, didn't your angry feelings eventually turn into lasting bitterness? Bitterness grew like a root toward that person who, in your mind, overshadowed you.

A drive then emerges to somehow get even, to strike back. Proverbs 6:34-35 tells it like this: " . . . jealousy enrages a man, and he will not spare in the day of vengeance. He will not accept any ransom, nor will he be content though you give many gifts" (NASB). Proverbs 27:4 reads, "Wrath is fierce and anger is a flood, but who can stand before jealousy?" (NASB). A prime example of this would be King Saul's murderous jealousy of David, discussed earlier.

As bitterness takes root toward the envied other, it normally grows toward a second object with as much tenacity as it did toward the first. I am referring to oneself. When beset with bitterness toward another, don't we end up feeling the same way toward ourselves as well?

Why? Self-directed bitterness emerges when one person lacks what the other is or has. It forms because of falling short and having to wallow in another's shadow. This bitterness can become so controlling and intense that one might resort to afflicting himself for the sake of retaliation. Let me illustrate. During my youth, I had a close friend, Pete, who had what is called a charismatic personality. And, in my mind, his was much more appealing and humorous than mine. I felt mine was rather dull by comparison.

Eventually my jealousy began to crop up toward Pete, causing my mind to fixate on his personality. Particularly when we were together, I dwelled on the obvious contrast between his personality and mine, much to the exclusion of positive, wholesome thoughts.

Consequently, anger swelled within, forcing me to fixate even more, leading to increased jealousy, and thereby closing the vicious circle.

Next, with this vicious circle remaining unchecked, my periodic bouts of anger turned into a solid root of bitterness toward Pete. Driven by a resulting instinct to get even with him, I began to emotionally cut myself off from him, which, one day, led to the sudden, unexplained termination of the relationship altogether.

Prior to this termination, though, I became embittered toward myself as well as Pete for falling, as far as personality was concerned, into his shadow. Then, agitated by my seeming deficiency, I became increasingly self-critical as a form of self-directed attack. Thus, when speaking of the havoc jealousy produces in the mind and relationships, I can speak painfully from personal experience.

I am thankful that since then God has encouraged and enabled me to be content and comfortable with the personality He has given me. I have learned that building Christlike qualities formed into Christian character is far more important.

As a result, I no longer compare my personality with others. Becoming like Christ is what's important, not cultivating a charismatic personality. So we can see why Paul readily identified jealousy as part of Satan's camp. Filling the mind with darkness, it shuts the door to the light that Christ longs to shine in.

Suggested Application. If you're jealous of someone, consider the havoc it will produce in your mind and relationships. Think of the described mental fixation, constriction of your field of consciousness, and bitterness held toward others and yourself that will come in its wake. What might happen to you if this green-eyed monster keeps you firm in its grasp?

Then engage in spiritual breathing. First, exhale. Confess the sin of jealousy to Christ. Do not try to justify or expect to gain from it. Confess it.

Next, inhale. Breathe in God's forgiveness. Allow the Holy Spirit to banish jealousy from your mind. Spiritual breathing complies with 1 John 1:9, which reads: "If we confess our sins, he is faithful and just and will forgive us our sins and purify us from all unrighteousness."

Having engaged in spiritual breathing, be sure to avoid temptations demanding the resurrection of jealous passions. Rather, "take captive every thought to make it obedient to Christ" (2 Corinthians 10:5), leading to a fortresslike stand against jealousy.

14
Don't Compare: You Are Custom-Made

One October day, a Mallard duck was floating in a stream when he was suddenly startled by loud honking sounds coming from above. Looking upward, he watched about fifty Canadian geese come into view, flying in perfect formation toward the South.

What a wonderful sight, thought the duck. *They fly so smoothly and with such power. Just look at their wonderful long necks—the richness of their colors—their markings—and their sounds! Just listen to the deep resonance of their honks!*

Simple admiration of the geese would have been OK. But the duck unwittingly did not leave it at that. He began to draw comparisons as well. "Oh, how I wish I could fly as well as they can. And to have a longer neck and their colors and markings. Wish I could sound like them, too. My dumb quack just leaves me cold!"

Thus, to excess, the duck magnified the splendor of the geese. But sadly, in the process, he lost sight of himself—his own special grace in flight—his richly colored green head, contrasted by earthtones in his feathers—his unique, special sounds. He lost sight of all of these in the name of comparisons.

Though the characters are unreal, the story's message is not. Destructive comparison-making is commonplace, permeating every segment of society.

An Old Testament example of this is seen in the lives of Rachel and her sister, Leah, both of whom were married to Jacob. For some time, God gave Leah sons, but Rachel remained barren, much to Rachel's distress. Drawing endless comparisons, she came to despise even life itself and cried out to Jacob: "Give me children, or I'll die!" (Genesis 30:1).

Skipping to the New Testament, during the Last Supper and immediately following Christ's forecast of His betrayal, His disciples were disputing "as to which of them was considered to be greatest" (Luke 22:24).

Reading between the lines, I sense that when the disciples learned of one less competitor, Judas, for spiritual supremacy, it triggered their comparison-making with the question: Who is the greatest disciple? Pride always does that, especially spiritual pride.

Drawing comparisons is as harmful as it is instinctive. It can open up a whole Pandora's box of ills. As the story about the duck shows, a person can fall into the trap of focusing on the strengths of someone else, while overlooking his own. He can become morbidly preoccupied with what is appealing about the other person, while suffering with a kind of amnesia to what he himself has to offer.

Then, as this dual fixation/blindness process continues, irrationality sets in. The person feels a strong pull to blow way out of proportion the other's assets. The other is seen as assuming a place of towering supremacy.

Naturally, as shown in the previous chapter, jealousy then emerges toward what the other person is or has, leading to bitterness toward the other and himself.

In family counseling, I have frequently seen this adverse pattern develop between siblings, especially when the parents unwittingly encourage rivalry. For example, several years ago, I came across a family in which there were two daughters, Chris and Guinn. Both girls possessed many good qualities. Among other things, Chris was expressive and personable while Guinn was concerned for others and self-disciplined.

Now at the age of sixteen, Chris drew the conclusion that her parents favored Guinn over herself. That idea activated endless comparisons on Chris's part. Caught in that trap, she fixed her attention on Guinn's good qualities while losing sight of her own. Worse still, Chris blew far out of proportion the appeal of Guinn's personality, giving Guinn a place of towering supremacy over her.

As expected, Chris then became increasingly jealous of Guinn. Her jealousy festered into bitterness toward Guinn and herself, precipitating endless power struggles between the two sisters. (I might add that this destructive pattern is especially seen in families where too much emphasis is placed on outward success as opposed to cultivating Christlike qualities.)

Hoping to combat harmful comparisons, Paul declared, "We do not dare to classify or compare ourselves with some who commend themselves. When they measure themselves by themselves and compare themselves with themselves, they are not wise" (2 Corinthians 10:12).

Paul saw Christ as the only one worth emulating, and we must believe the same. Certainly, His characteristics are manifest here and there in others, and seeing them sometimes spurs us on to change. But Christ is the only One ultimately worth modeling. Attempting this with anyone else is shortsighted and futile. Because many people use others as their ultimate reference points, their gaze is always horizontal, not vertical. They then employ humanistic standards to determine worth and value, giving rise to the adulation and glorification of abilities, looks, and personalities.

Moreover, because they do not take God seriously, many people remain in the dark about the fact that we were all created to be something special and unique. Then, in order to fill in the vacuum, they compare themselves, hoping to feel and look better than others.

Think again of the duck. Yes, the goose was clearly different with respect to flight patterns, colors, markings, and sounds. The two were easily distinguishable. But that does not mean that one was better than the other. Both were made into something special by their Creator, and the same applies to us.

To be sure, we all have different abilities, looks, personalities, and qualities. We were all made to be something special and unique. The more that truth sinks in and becomes a part of our minds, the less we will compare. And the less we compare, the more we can gaze upon others with love.

Suggested Application. If you're caught in the snare of making comparisons, it might result from your being blind to and ungrateful for what God has already provided. Out of a thankless heart you compare.

To make the necessary reversal of attitude, one possibility would be to keep a notebook called "God's Gifts" or "Gifts God Has Given Me." In it keep a running list of all that Christ has graciously provided.

On top of your list, write down the fact that God made you into a special, unique person. Then add all of those qualities and strengths He has been working overtime to build into your life. Include acts of love, family members, friends, opportunities, and other blessings.

Having launched this project, review your list once or twice each day. As you do, gratitude will well up inside you toward Christ for all of His gifts. Then you will lose your need and drive to compare.

15

Beware of Degrading Labels

"I say to you that everyone who is angry with his brother shall be guilty before the court; and whoever shall say to his brother, 'Raca,' shall be guilty before the supreme court; and whoever shall say, 'You fool,' shall be guilty enough to go into the fiery hell" (Matthew 5:22, NASB). Do you recognize the source and context of these blunt words? They were Christ's, spoken during His Sermon on the Mount.

Rather strong words, aren't they? And frightening, too, for who hasn't, at one time or another, employed the use of degrading labels in opposition to another? Who can possibly claim clemency from Christ's verdict?

Certainly, Christ issued those warnings among others during His famed sermon in order to drive home the truth that no one is worthy to enter God's kingdom on his own merits. Every person is in dire need of a substitute atonement, of a payment of sins on his behalf.

For those of us who identify with the cross, knowing Christ's underlying reasons behind such warnings takes away the sweat that is caused by them. Covered by His blood, we know we are safe from the wrath to come.

Nevertheless, we should not take any less seriously Christ's indignation against the use of degrading labels. We should not be any less cautious about using them. In fact, seeing our Father's grace and forgiving heart should compel us to be even more careful.

Look at the word *raca*. It is an Aramaic word, meaning something like "nitwit." Surely "raca" and "you fool" were illustrative in Christ's mind. Others could have been cited as well, for His righteous indignation is kindled against the use of any labels that degrade and depersonalize another human being.

The following scene depicts what I constantly run across in counseling sessions.

One day, Bob met with bitter disappointment at work. Outraged, he stormed home. Immediately, upon meeting his wife, Bob lashed out: "Jane, why didn't you get Danny to cut the lawn? You knew I've been on his case about this for days. You know, sometimes I think you're just plain stupid!"

A few hours later, Bob caught sight of Danny bursting through the door. "Danny!" he shouted at the top of his lungs. "Why didn't you cut the grass?! How many times do I have to tell you? You've just gotta be about the dumbest, most useless kid on the block!"

"Stupid," "dumb," "useless"—unfortunately, those were not the first times Bob mouthed such words. It was customary for him to do so whenever the pressure was on.

Someone might say, "I fail to see the harm in that. Why, just this past weekend, I called my daughter a 'jerk.' Words like that just don't bother her." Let me caution you. Such degrading labels probably do more damage than you realize. Because they have a branding effect upon the mind, they are very difficult to walk away from unscarred. Again, consider Bob and his family.

That day, although Bob quickly forgot about his labels, Jane did not. The sound of them continued to ring in her ears: "You're just plain stupid—you're just plain stupid—you're just plain stupid—"

With each repetition, the wound ran deeper. Feeling robbed of the consideration and respect due her, bitterness naturally sprang up inside Jane, creating an impenetrable barrier between her and Bob.

The next day, when Bob tried to compliment and embrace her, Jane recoiled inside, thinking, "Sure, *now* you want me to get all excited about your compliments! *Now* you want me to warm up to your embrace. But what about being called stupid, Bob? You can forget it!"

Along with Jane, Danny was damaged, too. Bob failed to see that the power of suggestion exercised by destructive labels can be great, especially for children.

In his penetrating book *The Strong and the Weak*, Paul Tournier warned, "To put a label on someone is inevitably to contribute to making him conform to the label, especially if the person is at the impressionable age of childhood."[1] And in another book, *The Meaning of Persons*, the same author said, "Call a child stupid, and you make him stupid, incapable of showing what he has it in him to do. . . . The power of suggestion exercised by the labels we are given is considerable. This is particularly the case in childhood, but the same is true throughout our lives."[2]

Thus, Bob's ill-chosen words, "You've just gotta be about the dumbest, the most useless kid on the block," stuck with Danny. With these words echoing in his mind that night, the next morning, and at school, he finally concluded, "If that's the way my dad looks at me, I must be dumb! I must be useless! So what difference does it make whether I try my best or not?"

Consequently, Danny began conforming to those labels. Feeling himself to be dumb and useless, he became apathetic, lazy, and uncooperative. Bob lashed out with such labels without restraint. Yet, they did not have to be reiterated in order to inflict damage. Once sometimes is enough. We can build a friendship for years. But mouthing something like "You're an idiot" or "You're worthless" just once can drastically change the complexion of that friendship for good. And, as seen in Jane and Bob's case, the same holds true for marriages.

Suggested Application. Christ commanded us to build others up, not to tear them down. That is why He expressed righteous anger over the use of "raca." Our words should stimulate others to be the persons God meant them to be, instead of placing them into boxes with degrading labels, thereby crushing them.

Whenever the temptation comes to strike someone with an offensive label, consider the long-term consequences. Think of the bitterness, the rift, and the possible change of complexion of that relationship. When children are involved, consider how they, impressionable and suggestible, are likely to conform to labels.

If circumstances call for corrective measures, select your words wisely so that the specific issues are attacked, but not persons. Employ words that stimulate change instead of backfire.

For example, in Bob's case, instead of pounding away with degrading labels, he could have said, "Jane, I'm bothered that you didn't remind Danny to mow the lawn. Sometimes you do forget.

---

1. Paul Tournier, *The Strong and the Weak* (Philadelphia: Westminster, 1976), 57.
2. Paul Tournier, *The Meaning of Persons* (New York: Har-Row, 1957), 50.

Let's figure out a way to help you remember, OK?"

Regarding Danny, instead of calling him dumb and useless, Bob could have said, "I'm disappointed that you did not mow the lawn. You know I've asked you all week to do it. Get it done by tomorrow, OK?"

See the difference? Instead of laying on labels that crush and demoralize, choose words that attack only the specific issue and stimulate growth.

16
Winning Isn't Everything

"Winning isn't everything; it's the only thing!" How often have you heard that expression? Particularly if you are a professional football fan, you have probably heard it from coaches and players alike. The high salaries for players—especially the "superstars"—the search for the best coaches, and the intense scrutinization process during the college draft all center on one thing: producing a winning season.

Winning not only lies at the heart of professional football, but the same philosophy permeates most segments of society. Students incessantly compete for the best grades. Workers compete for those positions holding the highest salaries and status. Stores and restaurants compete for customers.

True, a certain level of competition—this striving to win—is healthy and necessary. Among other things, it motivates people to grow and promotes our free enterprise system. Moreover, most of us enjoy either participating in sports or viewing athletes such as football players fiercely battling with each other. Nevertheless, the desire to win carries with it certain inherent dangers.

It can drive people to become obsessed with finding new sources of personal power, with fortifying their positions and status. Compelled by a "winning is the only thing" mindset, many are quite willing to crush others in their hot pursuits. They destroy their competition in overt or subtle ways, thinking that power builds with each crushing blow.

Can you think of any examples of this? What readily comes to mind is the man who crushes others while climbing the corporate ladder. With the ultimate goal of "Chairman of the Board" branded in his mind, he seeks to draw warm approval and promotions from his superiors. But, in doing so, he employs every tool available—including emotional blackmail, gossip, and lying—to eliminate competitors. He tries to make them appear foolish, incompetent, and sometimes even corrupt. Thus, step by step up the corporate ladder, he leaves human casualties along the way. You see, as far as he is concerned, "winning isn't everything; it's the only thing!"

You are probably coming up with other examples from your own experience. A person cannot miss this philosophy, since it is so integral to our system of doing things. More people function according to the "survival of the fittest" rule than care to admit it!

Consider other examples: the grade school bully who taunts and beats up smaller, weaker classmates in an effort to control their lives. The teacher who belittles her students for the same kind of twisted satisfaction a tyrant receives in ruling over his subjects. Or the brilliant university student who uses subtle, cutting remarks and a vast vocabulary to expose what he regards as the stupidity of fellow students.

Thankfully, Christ denounced gaining at the expense of others. He never denied the importance of success, so long as it complied with God's will. But the means used to reach our goals should never "intentionally" leave others injured along the way!

Thinking specifically of the Body of Christ, we are meant to work in constant mutual support and cooperation, like the parts of the physical body. We are exhorted to build, edify, encourage, and serve fellow believers, not elevate ourselves at their expense. Because every believer can be loved, become like Christ, and have a ministry, each of us has a chance to win at the same time. Unfortunately, power plays have cast their ugly shadows into the church as well as society, accounting for most of the squabbles and bitter divisions that have ripped us apart. Surely power struggles, while limiting God, delight the enemy of our souls.

Jan was a longstanding member of an evangelical church. For years she had wanted the chairmanship of the large women's group. However, blocking her way to "the top" were three other women, all gifted and proved leaders who shared her interest.

Distressed with reoccurring signs of opposition, Jan decided to eliminate the obstacles in her path. During group meetings, she was quick to oppose and subtly mock Joan's every proposal for new projects. When Mary, another competitor, was not around, Jan cut her down in front of others, pointing out all of her hang-ups and family problems. When Gail, the third opponent, was the topic of discussion, she dropped subtle but totally unfounded hints of her disloyality to the group. Does Jan remind you of anyone in your church?

What does Scripture say about this issue? Psalm 52 speaks of the mighty man who boasts in evil. "Here now is the man who did not make God his stronghold but . . . grew strong by destroying others!" (v. 7). Strong words. An indictment of many who call themselves Christians. The converse of this would be: those making God their stronghold avoid gaining strength by destroying others.

How pleasing Jan would have been to God if she had trusted Him to give her the desired position, if in His plans, and in His own way. Dignity and self-respect would not have waned, but increased. Moreover, Christ would have honored her labors by providing a fruitful ministry.

We need to ask ourselves: Though a believer, am I intentionally harming someone while pursuing any goals at church, home, school, or work? Instead of trusting God to provide the means to success, am I trampling others? If so, do I want to reverse this pattern and make God my stronghold?

Suggested Application. If change is needed, begin by asking Christ to reveal exactly how you are hurting others for the sake of personal power. Feedback may be required from those who are directly or indirectly involved, especially if you cannot see yourself clearly.

Then confess every wrongdoing to God. Be open, too, to Christ's possible leading to approach the offended parties and ask for their forgiveness. Needless to say, a change in behavior must accompany your confession.

Next, discern why you are trying to strengthen yourself at the expense of others. Commit this area of your life to God. Indicate that it is up to Him whether you advance as desired. If not, ask Him to supply you with alternative goals in compliance with His will. On the other hand, if you're given the green light, rely on Christ to provide the specific means to advance, knowing that, if you do it His way, others will not be trampled but strengthened.

17
Begin at Home

Picture in your mind the following two scenes. As you do, try to pick up a common theme.

Scene Number 1: Sally is pushing a grocery cart through a supermarket with her four-year-old daughter. Unexpectedly, she meets a long-time friend and becomes involved in a conversation, interspersed with smiles and laughter.

Finally, with the conversation ending, Sally catches a glimpse, out of the corner of her eye, of her daughter's hands clasped around a cereal box.

"Mommy, can we get this? Please?"

Feeling rudely interrupted, Sally grabs the box and snaps, "No, you can't have that. I've already picked the cereal. From now on, I don't want to hear another peep out of you."

Scene Number 2: Early Saturday morning, Jack meets with his friends at the usual golf course. Throughout the morning, walking from green to green, he tells jokes and humorous stories, entertaining everyone.

Afterward, Jack drives home. Upon arrival, he walks into the house, right past his wife and children, who were eagerly awaiting his return. Newspaper in hand, he settles into a comfortable chair.

Family members approach him, but Jack sends them certain cues suggesting that he is off-limits. Still feeling a need for him, his wife and children begin asking questions, only to be met with signs of discomfort and blank stares.

What do these scenes have in common? When visiting with people outside the family, Sally and Jack were both alert, attentive, and easily given to lively discussions and laughter. They were at their social best.

When interacting with family members, however, the whole climate of their personalities suddenly changed. With deflated interest levels, they were anything but their best selves with those closest to them. There was a distinct and obvious difference between their treatment of outside friends and of their family members.

You have probably witnessed this pattern. Maybe it occurs in your family. Such a dichotomy of behavior is especially destructive when a husband or wife exudes an aura of sainthood when attending church functions. Here, others are shown unlimited interest and warmth. However, his or her behavior is quite the opposite when at home. At any given moment, this same person can turn into an unapproachable bear, forcing family members to tip-toe around his or her feelings. Thus, the person at home contrasts sharply with the image projected at church.

Sue's father fell into this trap, forcing her into neurosis. For within Sue came a drive to withdraw from her father. The rejection she felt and the conclusion that those outside the family were more important than her, led to this drive.

Sue, however, also felt drawn to her father, compelled by a dire need for his approval and acceptance. Thus part of her was drawn to him while another part wanted to withdraw, setting up an intense inner conflict. And this unresolved conflict created great tension within Sue, resulting in bouts of emotional paralysis and then an inability to think clearly and make decisions. What accounts for such radical changes of behavior in and apart from home? Certainly, a number of factors, operating in isolation or motion together, can cause this dichotomy. But here are three major reasons.

First, with many, a carefully planned show or performance is put on for those outside the family, but they act just like themselves at home. These people fail to find real peace with themselves. Irritable and unfulfilled, they are discontent.

For the sake of being accepted and esteemed by the public, though, they hide what's really there and put on their best social selves. They protect themselves behind a shining social facade.

At home, however, this false pretense is shed, allowing their real miserable selves to gush out on family members. Minus the pressure of public opinion, the irritability comes back with a vengeance. Family members, therefore, are treated with less kindness and respect than outsiders.

A second major reason for the dichotomy is this: During the past few decades, a number of cultural, economic, and social forces have aligned themselves against the family, denouncing its importance and relevance. Swallowing that wicked premise, many have concluded that the family no longer deserves a person's best efforts. As a result, family members—children as well as parents—are forced to take a backseat to involvements outside the home—sports, work, social events, and sometimes even church activities.

Many believers, suggestible to society's twisted values, include God in their fantasy. They believe that He too is not as concerned with how the family is treated as those apart from it. This belief often emerges in the name of ministry. You see, in some people's minds, witnessing, raising money for missions, and serving on church boards are deemed "more important" than giving oneself to the family. But that is nonsense!

I am not suggesting that serving Christ outside the home is not important. Most assuredly, such service is vitally needed, and more Christians should give themselves to it. But the opinion that God esteems church activities more than the quality of treatment shown family members is both distorted and dangerous! Both kinds of service are important; both deserve our best efforts.

God is keenly alerted to and concerned with how family members are treated. And He feels both hurt and distressed when they receive the crumbs after others have got the meat.

God's concern is demonstrated in various parts of Scripture. For example, Paul listed a person's righteous management of his family as a major prerequisite to attaining the position of overseer: "He must manage his own family well and see that his children obey him with proper respect. (If anyone does not know how to manage his own family, how can he take care of God's church?)" (1 Timothy 3:4-5).

Back in the Old Testament, God's concern is seen through His reactions to two relationships in Jacob's life, those with his wife Leah and his Uncle Laban. As you recall, after fleeing for his life from Esau, Jacob came to live in Laban's household. Years later, after working for his uncle, he married Laban's daughters, Leah and Rachel.

Now Jacob loved Rachel, but not Leah. However, this short-sighted favoritism did not go unnoticed by God. In Genesis 29:31, the text reads, "When the LORD saw that Leah was not loved, he opened her womb, but Rachel was barren." God was keenly alerted to the harsh treatment shown to Leah. There was no indifference on His part to her wounded spirit. And God's compassion and sensitivity were shown by compensating Leah with precious children.

Consider Jacob's relationship with Laban. Laban was a trickster. He made it a regular practice to deceive Jacob, especially in regard to his daughters and Jacob's wages. But, as seen through Jacob's statement to his wives, such ill treatment did not go unnoticed by God: "I see that your father's attitude toward me is not what it was before, but the God of my father has been with me. You know that I've worked for your father with all my strength, yet your father has cheated me by changing my wages ten times. However, God has not allowed him to harm me" (Genesis 31:5-7).

Here again, God was neither oblivious nor indifferent to how one family member, Laban, treated another, Jacob. Rather, His mind's eye was keenly focused on the situation. And it interests me that God mercifully compensated Jacob for the way Laban tricked him, just as He compensated Leah for the way Jacob shunned her.

Thus, it is clear that the quality of treatment shown family members holds great concern to God. They must not be taken any less seriously than those outside the family. Our actions and words should instead be custom-tailored to edify them and to help them become all that God meant them to be. Family members deserve our best efforts.

Suggested Application. Carefully study Jacob's life upon entering Laban's household. It is depicted in Genesis 29-31. Scrutinize how Jacob, Laban, Leah, and Rachel interacted. Also try to capture how God was feeling and interacting through it all. As you do, it will become increasingly clear how deeply God feels about the treatment shown the family.

Coupled with this study, examine your own treatment shown your family members. Ask yourself: "On a scale from one to ten, how do I fare? How might I be hindering their growth, emotionally and spiritually? How could my efforts change to help bring out the best in their lives?" Then initiate the needed changes.

18
Don't Play Favorites in the Home

As you were growing up, did your parents seem to show partiality toward one child? Was one person considered "the favorite"?

"Yes," someone might respond. "My sister Sue was the apple of my parents' eyes. See, she got better grades than the rest of us. Always the most popular, too. And all of that was very appealing to my folks."

Another person might say, "Well, I guess I was considered 'the favorite.' I didn't mind it then. But looking back, I can see how it has hurt the whole family."

If partiality was shown in your family, you can probably identify with either the first or the second reaction. And if vivid memories of it flood back into your mind, they are probably charged with deep and perhaps raw emotion.

That is because a person normally cannot walk away from such an environment without strong feelings. Parents' playing favorites is an emotional issue, creating far-reaching effects upon each child, whether he was in the spotlight or not. Let's explore reasons for this, beginning with the children belonging to the "unfavored" camp.

Understandably, less favored children instinctively feel deeply wounded by their parents. You see, every child has a strong need to feel unconditionally loved and accepted by his parents. Every child must feel he's special and unique in their eyes.

Driven by these sensitive needs, the child then puts out "feelers" to detect exactly how his parents feel about him. Scrutinizing both verbal and nonverbal messages, he ascertains his standing with them, in contrast to those of his brothers and sisters.

Sadly, whether realistically or unrealistically perceived, the message he receives might be: "You are not as loved and important as your brother or sister. You just don't make the grade the way the other one does."

Mentally replaying such a message, the child feels cheated, robbed, and deeply wounded. Feeling betrayed by parents, he begins to build a resentment toward them, which, over a period of time, forms into bitterness. And that bitterness can be directed toward one or more of four possible objects.

First, logically, bitterness can emerge toward the parents for appearing brutally unfair. The reasoning might be: "Can't Mom and Dad see that their favoritism is tormenting me? They're so stupid, they can't see that I'm just as good!"

The second possible object of bitterness is the perceived "favored one." He is viewed by the unfavored as being either inferior or superior. If the favored is seen as being superior, the reasoning might go as follows: "Why can't I be more like Mary? She has everything going for her, but I'm just a dud. If I were like her, maybe Mom and Dad would think I'm OK, too. I can't stand her!"

If he's viewed as inferior, the unfavored might think: "Joe isn't as great as Mom and Dad think! Actually, I'm better! I'm superior. Why can't they see it my way?" Either way, the unfavored one comes away embittered, mentally revolting against the favored one.

The third possible candidate for bitterness is the person himself. Especially if inferiority feelings emerge, he grows to detest himself, to view himself as a worthless worm. Harsh self-accusations then arise for falling in the other's shadow, and for standing outside the sunshine of the parents' approval.

As the root of self-directed bitterness grows, it normally extends toward the fourth possible object: God. This occurs because there usually exists a close association between how a person sees himself and how he perceives God's creative powers. The reasoning goes like this: "I can't stand myself. I hate the way I was made. And that's where You come in, God. You sure blew it when You made me!"

Now, seething with bitterness toward one or more of the

described objects, the disfavored person strikes out at them, in an effort to get even. For example, if he is bitter toward his parents, he may punish them by contesting every verbal command they give him. Many have even plunged into the bizarre world of drugs as a means of sending the message: "Mom and Dad, you sure blew it when you raised me. Now suffer!"

Having examined the plight of the unfavored, let's briefly look at the favored. Although for some time he basks in the light of parental approval and blessings, someday he might realize that such treatment was not so good after all.

Finding himself in the limelight, he tends to view himself as better, or superior, than his brothers and sisters. And that attitude breeds smugness and self-satisfaction. He excessively compares himself with others, driven by the assumption that he will always win out. However, sooner or later, that backfires.

Eventually, others will come over the horizon, who are more athletic, intelligent, or popular. He will not always receive the highest esteem from coaches, employers, and teachers. And because his self-confidence and sense of value depended on basking in the spotlight in the past, feeling out of it comes as a crushing blow.

Consequently, depression and tension emerge, along with resentment toward others—especially the parents—for setting him up for failure in the real world. Thus, we can see how parents' "playing favorites" with their children damages the favored as well as the unfavored ones.

The story of Jacob and his sons provides a fitting example of this pattern. Joseph was born when Jacob was quite old. And soon he became his father's favorite: "Now Israel loved Joseph more than any of his other sons, because he had been born to him in his old age" (Genesis 37:3).

The text does not explain why Jacob's old age made a difference. Perhaps they spent more time together, since, by now, the older sons were working elsewhere. Or maybe Joseph most resembled Jacob's beloved wife, Rachel.

Whatever the reason, playing favorites was utterly foolish on Jacob's part. And he was even more shortsighted in the way he showed his preference, by making a multicolored tunic for Joseph.

Jacob should have known better. Having been considered the favorite himself by his mother, Rebekah, he had already witnessed the far-reaching consequences of such treatment. Among other things, his brother, Esau, had become murderously jealous of him. Jacob had been forced to flee from home for decades, never to see his mother again.

Noticing the coat as an obvious sign of Jacob's favoritism, Joseph's brothers erupted with bitter jealousy: "When [Joseph's] brothers saw that their father loved him more than any of them, they hated him and could not speak a kind word to him" (Genesis 37:4).

Consequently, Joseph's brothers decided to murder him. "They saw him in the distance, and before he reached them, they plotted to kill him" (Genesis 37:18). Fortunately, Reuben changed their minds, so they threw Joseph into a pit, instead. Then they sold their brother to Midianite merchants, who took him to Egypt.

Thus, driven by a consuming bitterness, the brothers struck out at Joseph in an effort to get even. They also sought vengeance against Jacob by harming his "beloved Joseph."

Think of Joseph. Though later in life he became very righteous, an Old Testament Christ figure, I sense that he was quite smug and self-satisfied as a youth. Joseph knew that he was his father's favorite. And he probably knew that wearing the beautiful coat would torment his older brothers. Knowing that, he should not have gloated over it and flaunted it, but he did.

I suspect that Joseph's arrogance was one reason, among others, that God allowed him to be thrown into a cruel Egyptian prison for a time. The imprisonment acted as God's refining tool on Joseph to humble him.

Thus, we can see why playing favorites on the part of parents is so brutal. Parents who play this deadly game find their family relationships exploding with bitter conflict.

Suggested Application. At the beginning of this chapter, I asked if you were raised in a home where partiality was shown. If so, have you ever become embittered toward your parents, the favored person, yourself, or God?

If you answered yes, I strongly encourage you to experience the liberation you need by undergoing the four steps described in chapter 2. Doing so might radically change the climate of your mind and your family relationships.

Turning now to parents, let me ask a question: Like Jacob, are you playing favorites with your children? If so, promptly correct yourself, because trouble will come if such treatment is continued. Like Jacob's sons, your children might become bitter and could be scarred for years, throwing your whole family into an uproar.

To make the needed change, begin by confessing your partiality as sin to God. Then, continuing in prayer, ask Him to help you gain a special concern and a new heart for the disfavored ones. Next, proceed to make adjustments so that favor and fairness are shown to all of your children, encouraging all of them to bask in the direct sunshine of your love.

19
Clothe Your Mind with Humility

Pride. Few people ever recognize this vice in themselves. Fewer still ever find lasting, permanent freedom from it. Yet, we are all quick to discover and then loathe pride in others. Perhaps there is no flaw that makes a person more unpleasant to be around.

Proverbs 16:18 states: "Pride goes before destruction, a haughty spirit before a fall." Pride can be lethal. It sets powerful forces of destruction into motion. Let's examine a few of them.

To begin, pride is obsessed with competition. It is consumed with winning, with always coming out on top in win/lose situations. Pride hungers to tower over others and to stand gloriously in the spotlight, forcing others into the shadows, even if that means beating them into the ground.

Pride is never content with just having something. It must have something more or better than the next person. The proud, for example, are not satisfied with having a good income. It must be higher than the incomes others receive. You see, with pride, it is the comparison that makes the difference.

Because pride is so obsessed with competition, it creates a lust for power. Power allows one person to control and manipulate other people at will. Seeking such power, pride tries to cast people into roles as puppets, thereby making them more predictable and less threatening. The proud love to pull the strings of others.

During my training period in the Army, I met a captain beset with deep insecurities and pride. Sadly, he took full advantage of his trainer position to satisfy his prideful appetites. His trainees frequently were forced to perform feats far beyond normal expectations, and much to his delight. One day, I was his target. This captain told me to fall on all fours on a wood floor and then do push-ups until he told me to stop. Up. Down. Up. Down. On and on I went for a seemingly endless time until a pool of water formed from sweat. With my hands slipping and agony in my face, I could see the captain was relishing it all!

Pride also distorts a person's perception of others. Committed to outflanking and overpowering others in win/lose situations, the proud hunt for their vulnerable points. (They search for weaknesses in order to exploit them.) So much time and energy are invested in this pursuit that the good qualities of others are either minimized or simply overlooked altogether, thereby distorting the prideful one's mental picture of other people.

Recognizing and then appreciating another person's strengths is difficult for the one who thinks he must be Number 1. As a result of the described forces of pride, the proud see others as "objects" to be dominated, not as persons to be accepted, encouraged, and loved. They use others to reflect their own self-induced glory.

Pride forces a person into contention with God. The proud person concludes that every success, or every good thing, finds its source in his own genius. He feels self-sufficient and capable of operating independently of God. He thinks and acts as if he were self-creating and self-sustaining. Such a mindset amazes me, because it is sheer self-delusion. We did not manufacture ourselves; God did. We do not even fully understand how our own bodies and minds work. But God does, because He made us. Therefore He alone deserves the complete credit.

We are all vulnerable. Every one of us, whether a ditchdigger or the President of the United States, is susceptible to danger. Accidents can happen suddenly. Certain mishaps with the brain or the heart can lead to instant death. The fact that everything can be here now and gone the next second testifies to our contingency.

It was pride that made Lucifer become Satan, the devil. His own pride would not allow him to be second to, or dependent upon, anyone but himself. One day, he chose to operate independently of God and even to compete with Him—his own Creator. Such was the height of Satan's arrogant self-delusion, as he tried to put himself above even the Lord God. The depths of his failure are obvious.

In sharp contrast to Satan's pride is Christ's humility. I am touched by the fact that though He is God, He is more humble than every person who ever lived. And he demonstrated that humility throughout His earthly existence.

Christ could have set foot on this planet robed with kingly apparel and announced by myriads of trumpeting angels. Yet He took the form of a child in a lowly stall. Philippians 2:5-8 reads: "Christ Jesus . . . being in very nature God . . . made Himself nothing, taking the very nature of a servant, being made in human likeness. And being found in appearance as a man, he humbled himself and became obedient."

At the onset of Christ's ministry, He did not invite the popular notables, the political and religious celebrities of the day, to be His intimate companions. He did not commission the men who would puff up His image in the eyes of people, but He chose common laborers. Fishermen.

Have you ever noticed that most people treat the rich, powerful, and well-known far differently than the poor, weak, and unknown? Associating with those belonging to the former group, they are their best selves—alert and enthused. Rubbing shoulders with those in the latter group, however, they act their worst selves—aloof and bored. Such contrasting behavior finds its source in conceit and an exaggerated sense of self-importance.

But Jesus Christ was different. He treated the poor, weak, and unknown the same as the rich, powerful, and well-known—with attentiveness, enthusiasm, kindness, compassion, sensitivity, and love. Humble, completely void of conceit, Jesus was at His best with everyone.

Just prior to Christ's crucifixion, "the men who were guarding Jesus began mocking and beating him. They blindfolded him and demanded, 'Prophesy! Who hit you?' And they said many other insulting things to him" (Luke 22:63-65). Imagine yourself standing there blindfolded with burly Roman soldiers slamming their fists into your face. I probably would have called upon every power at my disposal to crush them. But Christ, with His awesome powers, just stood there silently, humbly taking it all.

As a further evidence of Christ's humility, He is willing to take anyone into His eternal home (pending genuine repentance), even after everything else has been tried and failed. When I asked my wife, Karen, to marry me, I would have been rather disheartened to have been told: "Well, let me see where I stand with Pete, John, and Joe first. If they won't have me, then I'm yours!" It would have been terribly humiliating to have to accept Karen on those terms. Yet, Christ still accepts us, even after we have tried everything else. He is willing to be a last resort.

Thus, when God tells us to be humble, He is not prodding us to become something that He is not already, but rather something that He is. Colossians 3:12 reads: "As God's chosen people, holy and dearly loved, clothe yourselves with compassion, kindness, humility, gentleness and patience." First Peter 5:5 states: "Clothe yourselves with humility toward one another." We must make a choice: to strip off the stained clothes of pride and replace them with those colored with humility. Our minds must be clothed with humility toward God and other people.

That is why God sometimes allows us to undergo humiliating experiences. Those incidents burst our self-inflated balloons. They strip off our layers of pride, thereby removing our self-glorifying fantasies, so that we can begin to see ourselves more realistically.

Along with this, humility strips away our negative fantasies toward others. It replaces our searching for their worst with wanting to see their best. Of course, that does not mean that we become oblivious to their faults; that would be unrealistic. But we no longer cherish and exploit their weaknesses, as we did before. Instead, being humble and servant-minded, we gently help them to overcome their struggles. Thus, instead of being criticized, people are lovingly encouraged to become all that God meant them to be.

Moreover, a humble spirit acknowledges our creature/Creator relationship with God. We stop exalting ourselves with self-made, self-sufficient delusions. Instead, keenly aware of our contingency, and our complete dependence on God, we realize that He alone is worthy of being exalted. We become convinced that "Every good thing bestowed and every perfect gift is from above, coming down from the Father of lights, with whom there is no variation, or shifting shadow" (James 1:17, NASB).

Suggested Application. Clothing our minds with humility has to be an ongoing process. The temptation to puff ourselves up is ever-present, especially during times of success. Any one of us can succumb to it at any given moment.

In an effort to be humble-minded, I remind myself that every thought, every breath owes its existence to God. Always just a heartbeat away from death, all that I am and everything that I depend upon are wonderful provisions, gifts from God. I have also discovered that as God's grace—His unmerited acceptance and favor—has become more sufficient for me (see 2 Corinthians

12:9), my pride has gradually melted away. For as I have become more contented with and grateful for that grace, I have no longer desired to exalt myself, but only God.

That is one major reason the sufficiency of grace is so important to the Christian. Without it, a person's mental state of discontent would leave him vulnerable to prideful, self-serving cravings. Thus, in your effort to be humble-minded, I encourage you to explore the riches of God's grace.

As we become humble-minded, we gain fresh energy to live our lives joyously, as God intended, instead of battling to exalt ourselves, which only brings ruin. That is one reason C. S. Lewis said,

> He [referring to God] is trying to make you humble in order to make this moment possible: trying to take off a lot of silly, ugly, fancy dress in which we have all got ourselves up and are strutting about ... I wish I had got a bit further with humility myself: If I had, I could probably tell you more about the relief, the comfort, of taking the fancy dress off—getting rid of the false self, with all its "look at me." (*Mere Christianity*, p. 114)

20

Be Vulnerable: Tough Love Lasts

Have you ever felt compelled to show love in some tangible way, only to end up clutching inside? You felt a strong impulse to help another person or group. And you were about to take the plunge when something deep down inside of you cried out: "Don't do it! It could be risky. You could get hurt. Better play it safe."

"Last week," someone responds, "I wanted to offer counseling to someone who had a lot of emotional problems. I really wanted to help the guy out. But on went the brakes."

Another person says, "Recently, I was given the chance to work with the youth group in my church. At first, I was all excited about it. But then my doubts began working overtime. I answered no."

Why does this pattern occur? Often our love is restricted by our fear of getting hurt. We dread being vulnerable. The reasons for this dreaded vulnerability vary according to the perceived threats in each situation.

For example, while considering the idea of counseling a suffering friend, a person might fear a response like: "Don't you think you're being a bit pushy?" "Aren't you being somewhat presumptuous?" or, "What gives you the impression that I need counseling, anyway?"

The person who is asked to serve the church's youth might fear an inability to communicate, leading to their indifference and rejection. And because this fear poses too great a threat, he plays it safe and declines.

Having risked with and been hurt by past expressions of love, many people check themselves from venturing down that path again. They go to great lengths to avoid getting stung. Usually this is a bitter reaction. Determined, then, to protect themselves, those people construct shelters that, by design, keep them away from dangerous places. They erect walls to prevent them from crossing into vulnerable territory.

Here are three examples.

Shelter Number 1: Having been wounded in the past, some people convince themselves that they have little or nothing to offer to others. "So why even try?" they ask. For example, struck by a friend's rejection, one might conclude: "He didn't want my friendship. It probably wasn't good enough. From now on, the only one I aim to please is *me!* Who needs people, anyway?"

Shelter Number 2: Many play it safe by submerging themselves into a life of constant busyness. Whether it be at home or work, they set up unrealistic expectations for themselves, even if those expectations require evenings and weekends. Time simply does not permit intimacy.

Shelter Number 3: Many insulate themselves from the real needs, feelings, and pains of other people. They set up emotional barriers, allowing them to view others as objects, rather than persons.

We have all seen people in great need. But, committed to self-preservation, many people do not extend help to them. Instead of helping, they use rationalizations to justify their indifference: "That person wouldn't be thankful for anything I could possibly do. So why try?" Or, "There's so much suffering in the world. My puny efforts wouldn't even make a dent."

Who, in your mind, provides the best example in history of one who avoided shelters, who best exhibited vulnerable love? Undoubtedly, the best example is Christ. If ever a person had an opportunity to shelter himself, it was He. Safety was found in heaven. And refusing to cross into dangerous territory, He could have stayed there.

But, instead, Christ chose to become flesh, to plunge into our world torn apart by conflict and despair. To the Philippians, Paul said, "Although [Jesus Christ] existed in the form of God, He did not regard equality with God a thing to be grasped, but emptied Himself taking the form of a bond-servant, and being made in the likeness of men . . . He humbled Himself by becoming obedient to the point of death, even death on a cross" (Philippians 2:6-8).

Determined to flesh out His love, Christ became a man. But, while He did so, His foreknowledge told Him that He would bear, more than any other man, the pain of this world. Allowing Himself to be clothed with a human body—including a nervous system—Christ foreknew that excruciating pain would come from blows to His face by burly Roman soldiers, a crown of thorns on His head, and burning spikes in His hands and feet. By setting foot on this planet, Christ knew that Satan and his legions of darkness would take every opportunity to try to crush Him. He would experience unprecedented spiritual warfare, culminating in a hideous death on the cross.

But, hungry to reconcile, Christ met physical and spiritual horrors head-on. He courageously faced immeasurable sufferings, so that we might be transferred from the domain of darkness to the domain of His marvelous light (see 1 Peter 2:9).

Christ's love was committed, enduring, and tough! His love was not weak and wavering, but strong and persistent. And it is His full intent that our love become durable like His. For this reason, we will sometimes find ourselves placed into situations where our love is chiseled and refined.

For several years, I worked in a school for troubled youth, many of whom were delinquents. From the beginning, I heartily gave myself to them through endless individual, family, and group counseling sessions. Using skills that had lain dormant for years while I'd been in school, I enjoyed pouring myself into others.

I began to realize, though, that my help was not always welcomed with the same intensity as it was given. My help was all too often crammed back down my throat through cruel insults, cold indifference, and sometimes even physical assaults. Along with this nagging realization came a periodic drive to escape it all, to flee to safer ground.

Expecting Christ to sympathize with my predicament and lead me out of my bondage, my Egypt, I prayed for new direction. But none came. Instead, He kept telling me to endure, to stick it out, and to keep pouring out my love, even though doing so sometimes hurt. Yes, at times I expressed my hurt and pain as well as my anger to God and others. But this was far from running away.

Christ gave me the grace and strength to endure, and the results were clearly worth it. Many in our school were snatched from the jaws of crime, drugs, mental disorders, and rebellion.

Several young people were drawn into the kingdom, or closer to it. Moreover, Christ gave me a new understanding of what it means to flesh out His love.

The prodigal son's father (Luke 15:11-32) gives us a clear picture of the quality of love that Christ wants to build into our lives.

After losing everything through loose living, including half of his father's estate, the prodigal son found himself feeding pigs, just to earn his food. Then, finally coming to the end of himself and to his senses, he said to himself, "I will set out and go back to my father and say to him: Father, I have sinned against heaven and against you. I am no longer worthy to be called your son; make me like one of your hired men" (Luke 15:18-19).

Thus, in returning to his father, the son expected to be relegated to the place of a hired man, one who must earn the right to stay. But did his father see it that way? No, of course not. "While he was still a long way off, his father saw him and was filled with compassion for him; he ran to his son, threw his arms around him and kissed him" (Luke 15:20).

Have you ever been near a pig farm? Doesn't smell too good, does it? After living with pigs, the son smelled like them. And he had squandered everything. Yet, his father did not say, "Work in the fields and mend fences for seven months, and then I will accept you. Then I will love you." That would have been conditional love and acceptance—based on performance.

Instead, the father kissed him. Then he gave him a new robe, ring, and sandals. On top of this, a party was thrown to celebrate their joyous reunion. For his was unconditional love, enduring love, tough love—the kind that lasts.

If the story continued, I am sure we would see the son working hard in the fields and mending fences—not in an effort to earn his father's love, but out of deep gratitude for having received it as a gift already!

Suggested Application. Ask yourself: Have I constructed shelters for the purpose of protecting myself? Or, like Christ, am I willing to cross from places of safety to places of danger to flesh out His love? If your answers indicate a need for change in your life, begin by saying a prayer like the following one:

> Lord, You laid aside Your place of safety to enter our world of terror courageously and to show Your love. By doing so, You allowed Yourself to be hit with great testings and tribulations. Thank You. I now want to follow Your example. Give me the drive, courage, and power to step out of my self-made shelter. Place me into new situations where my love can become tough like Yours. Amen.

Having begun with such a bold prayer, allow the meat of it to become transformed into a heart-attitude, leading to a life-style of sacrificial love.

Christ will place you into new situations—sometimes raw situations—in which lives will be touched. You will find yourself in positions of great tension between God and Satan. But stick it out! Do not scramble back to your old shelter, because that would only turn into a smothering prison. Allow God's grace, His unmerited acceptance, to become sufficient for you (2 Corinthians 12:9). Let the joy of the Lord become your strength (Nehemiah 8:10).

To be sure, this will be a risky way to live. Standing in places of tension between Christ and the powers of darkness can sometimes be hazardous. But nowhere else will your love be toughened. And nowhere else will tough, enduring love be more explosive in effect.

21
Experience the Power of Small Groups

"The kingdom of God is the kingdom of right relationships." That statement struck me once while I was listening to a fascinating message. And since then careful study of the Scriptures has witnessed to that truth.

We are told to bear one another's burdens (Galatians 6:2), admonish one another (1 Thessalonians 5:14), and encourage one another (Hebrews 10:25). Moreover, we are exhorted to confess our sins to and pray for one another (James 5:16) and to stimulate one another to good works (Hebrews 10:24).

Yet relatively few Christians are complying with these biblical commands. Why? One major reason is that many believers simply do not know one another well enough to perform such tasks. Essentially, they are strangers. You see, I must draw close to another believer, go beyond our erected walls of defense, and see his burden before I can possibly bear it. A certain level of trust must be established before I can be free to admonish or correct him. A close bond must exist with another believer before I can feel comfortable confessing my sins to him. And that close bond depends upon intimacy created by honest sharing.

Unfortunately, because of the rigid structure of many churches, people are left with few or no opportunities to draw close enough to others on a regular basis for these functions to occur. Normally, when believers are gathered together, it is in large group settings where one or a few do most of the speaking. Others are too often cast into the role of spectators. And before and after such meetings, conversations seldom go deeper than a certain level.

Large group meetings are essential, especially on Sunday mornings when we gather to engage in corporate worship and to hear a message from God. But such meetings must be complemented by gatherings of much smaller units, in which deeper levels of sharing can occur. That is why I believe so strongly in Bible study, sharing, and prayer groups—those groups of people, two to twenty in number, that meet weekly in an informal setting to study the Scriptures, share, and pray for each other.

For several years, my wife and I have interacted in such small group settings, meeting in private homes. And we have found that the described interpersonal functions as well as others operate best in this context; the result has been obvious growth in our lives and those of others. Herein, we have gone beyond being mere strangers, or mere spectators, and interacted according to the New Testament's blueprint for personal relationships.

Church history bears witness to the power of small groups. Think first of Christ. The idea of the small group serving kingdom purposes began with Him. He set the pattern. Christ drew a band of twelve men close to Himself, in order to build intimacy, along with emotional and spiritual solidarity. This group, though small in number, was meant to provide the beachhead for Christ's invasion into Satan's domain.

The gospels tell about Christ's repeated interactions with huge, pressing crowds. Many of His messages were presented to thousands at a time. But this was balanced by meeting with the Twelve in private, intimate, small group settings, sometimes for extended periods of time.

That private setting, with informal teachings and genuine sharing, provided the best-suited environment for the building and healing of the disciples' minds and relationships, making them into formidable foes against the kingdom of darkness. Christ set a good precedent for us to follow.

The early church quickly caught on to Christ's strategy. In addition to meeting in large groups to hear the apostles' teachings, believers also broke down into small cells. In fact, during the first two centuries of the church's life, they met almost exclusively in private homes, not in catacombs as supposed. Acts 2:46 reads: "Every day they continued to meet together in the temple courts. They broke bread in their homes and ate together with glad and sincere hearts."

The Greek word *koinonia* depicts the quality of fellowship experienced by the early church. The term embodies concepts of communion, deep sharing, and partnership. *Koinonia* took place in large groups, but more effectively in smaller ones in homes. To the Roman Christians, Paul said, "Greet also the church that meets in [Priscilla and Aquila's] house" (Romans 16:5).

It was in a small group that George Whitefield and Charles and John Wesley met to share and grow. Here, operating as a team in a hostile Oxford environment, these men formulated many of their aspirations that played significant roles in their revolutionary ministries thereafter.

For decades, John Wesley found his messages meeting with great success, as he addressed five, ten, or sometimes twenty thousand people at a time. Knowing, however, that great preaching, by itself, does not beget spiritual maturity, Wesley immediately began gathering people into societies. Varying in number, the societies encouraged, safeguarded, and trained the people.

Soon the societies were broken down into much smaller units: class meetings and bands. The class meeting, which normally held between twelve and fifteen people, became the heart of Wesley's movement. Each neighborhood centered in close proximity to a wise leader; here people discussed their spiritual progress, including personal needs and struggles. Such discussions gave rise to exchanges of advice and encouragement. Wesley commented, "Advice or reproof was given as need required, quarrels were made up, misunderstandings removed: And after an hour or two spent in this labour of love, they concluded with prayer and thanksgiving."[1]

Class leaders came from many different backgrounds and occupations: the rich and poor, the educated and uneducated, bakers, blacksmiths, cobblers, and so on. Wesley knew that wise discernment and true spirituality, not socio-economic status, were the best qualifications for spiritual authority and leadership. Each class leader served as a shepherd of his group, giving personal intimate care and oversight.

Wesley commented on the effectiveness of such groups:

> It can scarce be conceived what advantages have been reaped from this little prudential regulation. Many now happily experienced that Christian fellowship of which they had not so much as an idea

1. John Wesley, *Works of John Wesley,* 14 vols. (Grand Rapids: Baker, n.d.), 8:253-54.

before. They began to "bear one another's burdens" [Galatians 6:2], and naturally to "care for one another" [1 Corinthians 12:25]. As they had daily a more intimate acquaintance with, so they had a more endeared affection for, each other. And "speaking the truth in love, they grew up into Him in all things, who is the Head, even Christ." [2]

For decades Wesley labored to build the class meeting network with thousands throughout England. It was primarily those close-knit fellowships that kept the flame of England's spiritual awakening alive for years.

Along with the class meeting, another smaller unit came into existence, called "the band." Containing between four and ten (on the average, six) members, the bands were designed to encourage even deeper levels of sharing between believers. Wesley observes,

> These [new Christians] wanted some means of closer union; they wanted to pour out their hearts without reserve, particularly with regard to the sin which did still easily beset them, and the temptations which were most apt to prevail over them. And they were the more desirous of this, when they observed that it was the express advice of an inspired writer: "Confess your faults one to another, and pray for one another, that ye may be healed." [3]

This intimate group stressed confidentiality, encouraging members to shed masks and false pretenses and to reveal their real selves. Personal flaws, sins, and temptations were openly admitted and discussed. The result was great personal and interpersonal healing among the members of the group.

One woman who experienced such healing wrote to Wesley: "We find great power from the Lord in our own private band, the love of God shed abroad in our hearts, our souls knit to one another, we drink of one spirit and the Lord doth meet us." Such a therapeutic role was imperative, since major population shifts with developing industry were tearing up the roots and stability of thousands.

These societies, class meetings, and bands kept the spiritual awakening in England going for decades. For here, in sharp contrast to the cold formality of the Church of England, intimacy and tough love emerged, fleshing out the essence of God's kingdom.

Whenever small groups are taken seriously, the resulting benefits are great. Mighty advances are made. Let's explore several of them.

2. Ibid., 254.
3. Ibid., 258.

To begin, the small group satisfies our God-given need for self-expression. Built into each one of us is a strong drive to express our struggles and our triumphs. Compelled by this drive, many approach the church but sadly do not find any place where their deepest feelings and thoughts are legitimate topics for discussion. In fact, they discover that the local church is often the last place where people talk freely about what touches them most. What many find instead is an amazing lack of basic honesty. Consequently, many choose bad substitutes—like bars and taverns—to reveal themselves. The substitutes they choose, incidently, are counterfeits, imitations of what the church ought to be.

This, again, is where the small group comes in. Here, the basic need for self-expression and revelation can be joyously and effectively met. In a spirit of love, people can share their deepest longings with each other, thereby building intimacy and unity.

Second, as group members speak their minds in a spirit of love, our masks or false pretenses are shed, exhibiting our strengths and weaknesses. As a result, we become increasingly more honest with ourselves, God, and others. Moreover, no longer pretending to be something we are not, our minds become clothed with humility toward God and others, enabling us to more freely love them.

Third, as a result of stripping off our masks and exposing our struggles, we are in a much better position to obtain help. Other group members can offer us the encouragement, wisdom, and love that we need. Their petitioning prayers can bring healing to our minds and relationships, complying with James's instruction "Confess your sins to one another, and pray for one another, so that you may be healed" (James 5:16, NASB). As a group, we are better able to tap into the many rich resources offered by Christ.

Fourth, once a person dares to reveal his sins and weaknesses, as well as his strengths, and discovers that he still receives acceptance and support from group members, he can more readily conclude that God and others truly love him. The reasoning is as follows: "Even though they know my sins and weaknesses, they still love and accept me. This must be for real. God must truly love me, too!" It is my firm belief that many people will never grasp and trust in God's unfailing love unless they go through that process first.

The fifth benefit of small groups concerns spiritual gifts. Paul lists and describes the many spiritual gifts (1 Corinthians 12:1-11) and states that every Christian has at least one of them. Every believer's gifts and contributions are important and vitally needed by the rest (see 12:12-26). The small group provides one of the best settings for discovering and employing those gifts.

Gifts of discernment, exhortation, helps, mercy, teaching, and wisdom, along with others, operate very well in the small group. For example, the believer entrusted with the gift of exhortation is provided with many fresh opportunities to encourage other group members after discovering their challenges, pains, and struggles exposed by honest sharing. And as a result of exercising our spiritual gifts and profiting from those of others, we gain fresh power to live for Christ.

Sixth, small groups offer strategic places for personal evangelism. During the past several decades particularly, great evangelistic thrusts have occurred through local church ministries, radio, television, and mass crusades. Millions have been reached for Christ. However, many more millions have not even been touched.

Many unbelievers stubbornly resist setting foot into church buildings, much less participating in their activities, because of painful memories or stereotyped impressions. Many of those same people, however, would respond favorably to an invitation to sit in on a small, informal group meeting in a friend's home. Most likely, they have already found that home to be a place where they can relax, open up, and speak their minds.

Then having entered the group, caught in a cross fire of loving acceptance, the unsaved can be drawn into the kingdom. Listened to, encouraged, and unconditionally loved, they get a good taste of God's home, compelling them to give their lives to Christ.

What excites me is that the same group can then assume a discipling role in the new believers' lives, something that many other modes of evangelism, with their inherent limits, cannot pull off. Because of the dual role of the small group—evangelism and discipleship—this approach provides one of the best strategies for communicating the gospel and building disciples.

Seventh, because of the described benefits and others, the small group can mobilize believers for outreach. As we grow emotionally, socially, and spiritually and discover and use our spiritual gifts, we are better prepared to serve those apart from the small group. The group acts as a solid base, launching us into new orbits of adventure for Christ.

This happened to the Twelve. After months of encouraging, loving, teaching, and discipling them, Jesus began to thrust them into dynamic ministries. The disciples were sent out two by two to heal, cast out demons, proclaim the gospel (Mark 6:7-13), and then return to the group for fresh support. Their small group gave them a firm base, launching them into new ministries.

This same strategy was seen in Wesley's bands and class meetings. As peoples' minds and relationships were healed in such groups, they gained new freedom and drive to make an impact apart from the group. Here, upheld by God's grace, their minds became girded for action (1 Peter 1:13).

Social ills concerning child labor, the homeless, inadequate medical care and schooling for the poor, slavery, and other issues were courageously attacked, causing a great reform of society. It was that bold movement, more than anything else, that saved England from its own version of the bloody French Revolution. Thus, we can see that the small group can play a significant role in our lives. Given our world's economic, moral, and social upheaval and decay, the small group's impact is vitally needed for today.

Yes, dangers do exist. The group can become ingrown, turning into a small clique, gossip corner, or gripe session. It can regress into a mere social club, ignoring the vitally needed vertical relationship with Christ. The group can also place too much emphasis on feelings and personal experience, at the expense of investigating and applying sound biblical principles.

So dangers do exist. But the rich possibilities far outweigh the risks. And the group that truly hungers and searches for Christ's guidance and righteousness will see those possibilities realized, resulting in great gain.

Today, many believers feel comfortable being emotionally separated from others. They like being self-sufficient. But I do not expect that pattern will continue. Great economic, moral, and social pressures are creating an atmosphere of fear, instability, and insecurity. And such conditions will force more and more believers to recognize their need for each other—for giving and receiving greater expressions of love and mutual commitment. They will be compelled to plunge into small, warm fellowships, hoping to withstand the increased stress-loads of the day.

The Body of Christ must move now to awaken itself to the dire need for small groups and then proceed with wisdom to establish them. If not, I fear that many within the ranks will fall prey to the jaws of adversity.

Suggested Application. If you have not done so already, plunge into an existing small group. Become part of a group in which the members speak honestly with each other and where plenty of understanding, support, and love are shown. Ask Christ to direct you to a group that is custom-tailored for you. ,

It is even possible that Christ wants you to start a group of your own in your home, school, or place of employment. Be in prayer about this, especially if God has equipped you with spiritual maturity and gifts fitting for this role.

Then, if God gives you the green light, ask Him to bring the right people into your group. As you meet, cut your time into three blocks for studying the Scriptures, sharing, and prayer. The proportions given to each will depend upon the specific needs and established goals of your group.[4]

Throughout these pages, I have examined how minds and relationships can be healed. The small group offers a wonderful setting in which Christ's power can be unleashed for healing, animating us with tough love for God and others.

---

4. For more information on launching and building a group, read: *Small Groups: Getting Them Started/Keeping Them Going*, by Michael Wiebe. Published by InterVarsity Press, this booklet is filled with helpful insights and suggestions. Toward its end is a bibliography, suggesting books for further small group study.